Beware the coast of Ireland

Sam Hutchison

Wordwell

To my son George and the men and women of the Air–Sea Rescue Service

First published 2013
Wordwell Ltd
Unit 9, 78 Furze Road, Sandyford Industrial Estate, Dublin 18

ISBN: 978 1 905569 77 9

British Library Cataloguing-in-Publication Data.
A catalogue record for this book is available from the British Library.

Typeset in Ireland by Wordwell Ltd.
Copy-editor: Emer Condit.
Book design: Nick Maxwell.
Printed by Castuera, Pamplona.

CONTENTS

PREFACE

'O hear us when we cry to Thee
For those in peril on the sea'
—William Whiting (1825–78)

Ireland is a small country with a remarkably long and indented coastline of almost 5,000 miles (8,000 kilometres). For much of its length it is beautiful and romantic, with dramatic cliffs, mountains tumbling down to the sea, glorious sandy beaches, delightful bays and coves with welcoming harbours and a necklace of charming islands. When the weather is fine and sunny and the sea calm there is no better place to be. On such a day it is difficult to imagine the dramas that have unfolded over the centuries along this seaboard and the unknown number of lives lost in disasters of every kind. Documentary evidence alone tells us of at least 15,000 wrecks, almost all hidden from our view. One of the few exceptions is the cargo ship *Plassy*, which was wrecked and beached on Inisheer Island on 8 March 1960 and is well known as part of the title sequence of the *Father Ted* television comedies. The islanders came swiftly to its aid and all eleven crewmen were winched safely ashore.

Strangely, for islanders living on the edge of a great ocean, the majority of Irish people do not have a great relationship with the sea or maritime affairs, nor has any government since Independence done much to encourage an interest in naval matters. This extends to happenings off our coast, which should be better known—for example, the fact that the Spanish Armada in 1588 suffered greater casualties and lost more ships along the Irish coast than in all their battles with the English. The worst shipping disaster in the Irish Sea, the sinking of the Dublin mail steamer *Leinster* in 1918, is barely remembered. The same is true of the 135 seamen who were killed in Irish merchant ships during the Second World War. This book attempts to elaborate on these events and other marine tragedies on or in close proximity to the shore. Some, like the sinking of the liner *Lusitania*, are of historical significance, but most are stories of great storms, hardship in the days of sail, total war, endurance, bravery, incompetence and negligence involving ordinary people but, in particular, those who go down to the sea in ships or do their business in great waters.

The investigation and archaeology of wreck sites is beyond the scope of this book, but much work has been carried out in the past 50 years and the process is ongoing. The *Shipwreck Inventory of Ireland: Louth, Meath, Dublin and Wicklow* compiled by Karl Brady is a good example of what has been achieved. The permanent exhibitions in the Ulster Museum in Belfast on the Spanish Armada vessel *Girona* and in the Tower Museum, Londonderry, on the *La Trinidad Valencera* from the same fleet display a huge variety of artefacts, ranging from cannon to delicate items of jewellery. These are the result of patient and painstaking dives over a long period of time, with the work of the Belgian Robert Stenuit and his team on the *Girona* site especially worthy of mention. Important wrecks in Dublin Bay and the surrounding area are regularly visited by divers and many interesting artefacts have been brought ashore.

I would like to thank the many people who helped me during my research and visits to wreck sites, as well as those who supplied illustrations, paintings and photographs—in particular the National Library of Ireland, the National Maritime Museum, Greenwich, the National Museum Northern Ireland and the Merseyside Maritime Museum, Liverpool. The Dundrum and Stillorgan Libraries in County Dublin were also of great assistance.

Finally, my best thanks to Alison Law for typing my scribbles so accurately and in such a competent and cheerful manner.

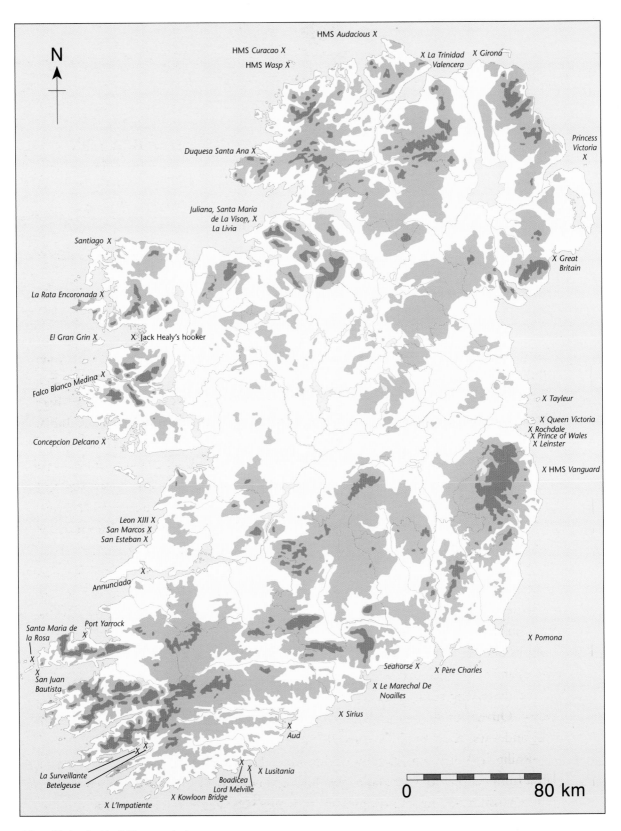

N

HMS *Audacious* X

HMS *Curacao* X
HMS *Wasp* X

X *La Trinidad*
Valencera   X *Girona*

Princess
Victoria
X

Duquesa Santa Ana X

Juliana, Santa Maria
de La Vison, X
La Livia

Santiago X

X Great
Britain

La Rata Encoronada X

El Gran Grin X   X Jack Healy's hooker

Falco Blanco Medina X

X Tayleur

X Queen Victoria
X Rochdale
X Prince of Wales
X Leinster

Concepcion Delcano X

X HMS *Vanguard*

Leon XIII X
San Marcos X
San Esteban X

X
Annunciada

Port Yarrock
X

X Pomona

Santa Maria de
la Rosa
X

X
San Juan
Bautista

Seahorse X   X Père Charles

X Le Marechal De
Noailles

X *Sirius*

X
Aud

X X

La Surveillante
Betelgeuse

X X
Boadicea   X *Lusitania*
Lord Melville
X Kowloon Bridge

X L'Impatiente

0   80 km

Map of Ireland with sinkings marked.

The graveyard of the Spanish Armada

'Take great heed lest you fall upon the island of Ireland for fear of the harm that may happen to you on that coast'

—the duke of Medina Sidonia.

In the sixteenth century Spain was the greatest power in Europe. In 1588 its king, Philip II, ruled a larger empire than any other in history up to that time. It included Portugal, Sicily, Naples, Milan, parts of France and the Netherlands. Overseas there were huge domains in south and central America and enclaves in Africa and India. Further east were the Philippine Islands, named in his honour. This was not only a political empire but also a religious one; King Philip, a fanatical Catholic, believed that he had been appointed by God to punish Protestants and unbelievers everywhere and to rescue Catholics who lived under Protestant rule. In this he succeeded in every part of his empire with the exception of the Netherlands, where for the previous twenty years a large and experienced army had failed to put down a Protestant revolt.

One reason for the failure was the assistance given to the Dutch by England's Protestant Queen Elizabeth. At the same time she was turning a blind eye to the activities of her seamen, many of whom were making piratical voyages to rob the Spanish treasure ships bringing home gold and silver from the Americas. The most famous of these was Sir Francis Drake, who in 1578 entered the Pacific Ocean, which the Spanish king claimed as his own, for the purpose of plunder; in 1587 he raided Cadiz, destroying many ships and doing great damage. In the same year the Catholic Mary Queen of Scots—in Philip's view the legitimate heir to the throne of England—was executed by Elizabeth.

Philip had been considering an invasion of England for a long time and these latest humiliations convinced him that he could postpone it no longer. Indeed, he saw it as a mission that he had received from God. At his command a great fleet of 130

Medina Sidonia's flagship, the *San Martín*.

ships, known as 'the Enterprise of England', was assembled in Lisbon, and in May 1588 it set sail with over 8,000 sailors, 19,000 soldiers and 2,400 guns. He appointed as commander-in-chief a leading member of the Spanish nobility, the duke of Medina Sidonia, who had little experience as a soldier and no seafaring background. The duke genuinely felt unequal to the task and told the king so, but the latter was adamant that he accept. The plan for the entire project was devised solely by the king, whose subordinates were expected to follow it to the letter. In simple terms, the Armada (from the Spanish *Armata*, meaning 'army') was to sail to the English Channel and destroy the English fleet. It was then to go to the straits of Dover, where it would liaise with the duke of Parma, commander-in-chief of Philip's army in the Netherlands, who would supply additional ships and soldiers. The entire force would then sail up the Thames, capture London and subdue the rest of the country. With God on his side and the cause so just, the king felt assured of a splendid victory.

The Armada was plagued by misfortune from the beginning. Just a few miles from Lisbon, a strong head wind forced it to anchor at the mouth of the Tagus, and there it stayed for sixteen days before the wind shifted and enabled it to put to sea. Not long afterwards came a series of gales, which first forced the fleet towards Africa and then north again. Ships became separated and many suffered damage. As a result, the whole fleet was forced to seek refuge in the port of Corunna in north-west Spain, where repairs were carried out and fresh stores taken on board. It was not until 22 July, 73 days after its departure from Lisbon, that it was ready to go to sea again.

Seven days later it was off the coast of Cornwall and began a dramatic passage along the shores of England, as demanded by the king; the coast of France would have been much safer. Almost immediately it was attacked by the English fleet and running battles ensued for the next week, none of which were decisive despite a huge expenditure of powder and shot by both sides. Two Spanish ships were put out of action, the English lost none and casualties in both fleets were remarkably light. The Armada was in serious trouble, however, because Medina Sidonia had received no response to the many messages sent to the duke of Parma to confirm the date and place of their rendezvous. As no invasion could be contemplated without Parma's aid, the Armada was forced to anchor off Calais in Flanders to await developments. This was a fatal error and one that the English quickly exploited.

Fire-ships were a very potent weapon against wooden warships at anchor. Within a few days the Armada was attacked by eight of them in line abreast but managed to escape without loss by cutting its cables. It was, however, put to flight and the 300 anchors left on the seabed would be sorely missed. The ships were again scattered and immediately attacked by every available English warship. The ensuing Battle of

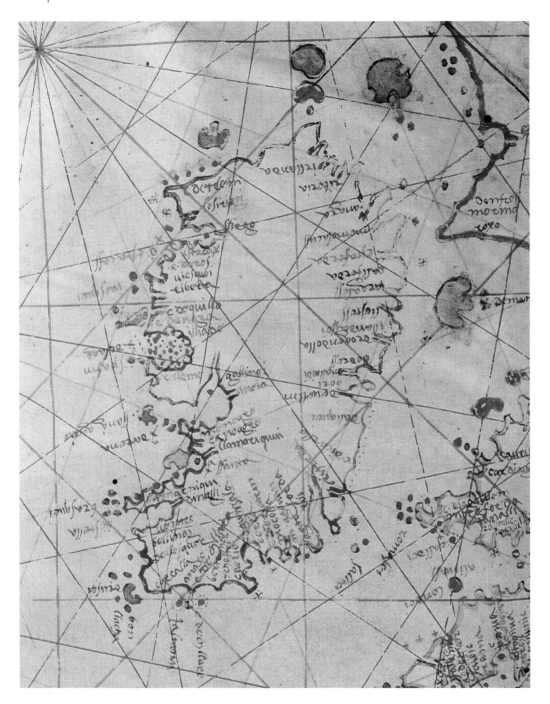

A sixteenth-century map of Ireland by the Flemish cartographer Ortelius, who visited the country in 1577.

Gravelines was the death-knell of the Armada, although this was not realised at the time. Only eight Spanish ships were sunk or captured, but serious damage had been done to many others owing to the greater manoeuvrability of the English ships and their superior rate of fire. Medina Sidonia realised that all was lost and fled northwards. His only chance of returning safely to Spain was to sail around England, Scotland and Ireland, and the Armada headed into the North Sea in as good an order as possible, harried by the English as far as the Firth of Forth. It was clear at this stage that the Armada had given up all thought of invasion and was on a course for home.

On 16 August, in good weather, it sailed between the Orkney and Shetland Islands near Fair Isle and began the 1,500-mile journey to northern Spain and safety. To the astonished islanders the Armada must have been an amazing and impressive sight, with over 100 ships still at sea. For those on board, however, life was a constant misery, especially for the thousand and more badly wounded on those ships which had borne the brunt of the fighting. Scurvy and typhoid were rife, food rotten, water scarce and vermin everywhere. The foul stench of vomit and excrement was a constant presence. Those who suffered most were the huge numbers of soldiers who, for almost three months, had been crammed below decks, except when called upon to fight. They had only been ashore once—on an island near Corunna to confess their sins and seek absolution. This was the fleet that Medina Sidonia now ordered to sail directly to Spain out of sight of land. He especially warned his captains to avoid Ireland 'for fear of the harm that may befall you upon that coast'. Many captains could not follow this good advice, however, as their ships were breaking up and in need of urgent repair. Many Armada vessels were built for use in the Mediterranean and were not strong enough to withstand the dreadful storms they had encountered in the north Atlantic. Most had also suffered damage during the fighting. On board were thousands of men in a poor physical state, close to starvation and in urgent need of fresh food and water. When they headed for Ireland they must have expected a reasonably warm welcome from the natives and the opportunity to take on board enough supplies to see them home. This would have been an understandable attitude, bearing in mind that the Irish had, for decades, been seeking help from Spain against their common enemy. The reality turned out to be somewhat different.

In the middle of September 1588 the sudden appearance of scores of 'Great Ships' struck terror into the English garrisons along the west coast from Donegal to Kerry. News of their arrival soon reached the lord deputy, Sir William Fitzwilliam, in Dublin. He immediately feared an invasion, which his meagre forces would have great difficulty in opposing, especially if supported by the Irish clans. He issued immediate and strict orders to the governor of Connacht, Sir Richard Bingham, and

Dunluce Castle, Co. Antrim, where Armada survivors received a warm welcome from the Ulster chieftain Sorley Boy MacDonnell.

other officials that any Spanish who came ashore were to be slaughtered without mercy and prisoners executed. The same applied to any Irishmen who came to their aid. In hindsight such instructions appear barbarous, but at the time the English did not realise that the Armada was in such disarray, nor were they aware of the desperate situation of those on board. From their point of view, these ships posed a huge threat to English rule in Ireland and they feared the worst.

Among the first to arrive was the *La Trinidad Valencera*, a Venetian galleon and one of the largest in the Armada. Its commander was an experienced soldier, Don Alonzo de Luzon. On 12 September she was hit by a severe storm and, leaking heavily, headed for the mouth of Lough Foyle in County Donegal. Shortly afterwards she struck a reef in Kinnagoe Bay, and two days later broke up and sank. Some 400 men, including survivors of the *Barca De Amburg*, which had sunk a week or so earlier, were helped ashore by the O'Doherty clan, whose chief, Sir John O'Doherty, persuaded them that their best course of action was to march to County Antrim, which was almost free of interference by the English at that time, and seek passage to Scotland. This was a daunting prospect for de Luzon and his worn-out and demoralised men, but he had little choice and set out bravely on the first stage towards Derry, with drums beating and banners flying. It is not clear whether Sir John, who was supposedly loyal to Queen Elizabeth at this time, was genuine in his desire to help or whether he led the Spaniards into a trap, but as they approached one of his castles after three or four days' march they were confronted by 200 mounted soldiers, who demanded their surrender. These were not English soldiers but Irishmen in the pay of England, commanded by a Major Kelly and brothers Richard and Henry Hovenden, cousins of the earl of Tyrone. They parleyed for two days and de Luzon finally submitted, following a promise from Kelly that his entire party would be brought safely to Dublin and thence to England. As soon as the soldiers laid down their arms, however, they were stripped naked and cold-bloodedly attacked by Kelly and his cavalry, leaving nearly 200 dead. An indeterminate number managed to escape with help from the bishop of Derry, and eventually reached Scotland thanks to Sorley Boy MacDonnell of Antrim and O'Cahan of Dungiven. The remainder—including de Luzon, his officers, priests and gentlemen—were then marched to Dungannon and from there to Drogheda, a distance of over 100 miles, where they were 'interrogated', a term that often involved torture. By 1591 only de Luzon and another officer are known to have survived, and it is believed that both eventually returned to Spain following a prisoner exchange.

On 20 September three large ships entered Donegal Bay, driven there by strong westerly winds. To avoid shipwreck they anchored one and a half miles off Streedagh

The Armada attacked by English fire-ships while at anchor off Calais.

beach, which is about ten miles north-west of Sligo town. They were the Castilian galleon *Juliana*, the vice-flagship of the Levantine squadron, *La Livia*, and another Levantine ship, the *Santa Maria de la Vison*. On board were an estimated 1,300 men. The winds persisted for four days and on the fifth grew worse. Almost simultaneously the anchor cables parted and all three ships were dashed on the shore, where within an hour they were broken to pieces. Many of those on board were drowned or so badly injured that they could not get ashore, but hundreds staggered onto the beach, where they were cut down by soldiers from the English garrison in Sligo. Others were attacked by the local Irish, who, more interested in plunder, stripped the dazed men naked, taking all that they owned. Some struggled free and escaped inland; the rest were hunted down and executed. Fitzwilliam visited Streedagh strand later in the year and heard that 'not long before over 1000 dead bodies lay there', whilst he saw 'as great a store of timber of wrecked ships as would have built five of the greatest ships that I ever saw'. This was one of the two most horrifying shipwrecks suffered by the Armada in Ireland.

It is estimated that as many as 60 Armada ships passed close to the coast of Ireland. Five of these came to grief off the shores of County Mayo during the storms that raged during the third week of September. The largest and most important was the *La Rata Encoronada* of the Levantine squadron, into which about 600 men were crammed, including 60 or so from some of the noblest families in Spain. In command was Don Alonzo de Leyva, one of Spain's finest and bravest soldiers and the man appointed by King Philip to replace Medina Sidonia if the latter died. The *Rata* was in very poor condition and lacked its principal anchors, which it had left at Calais, when it anchored off Fahy Strand in Tullaghan Bay on 21 September. That night she began to drag and at dawn grounded on the beach and became immovable. It soon became evident that she could not be refloated, and the men came ashore with such valuables as they could carry. The *Rata* was then set on fire and destroyed. Another, larger ship, the *Duquesa Santa Ana* of the Andalusian squadron, had anchored safely in Etty Bay (part of Blacksod Bay) to the north, and de Leyva realised that their only hope of safety was to join her. This meant a march of 25 miles through wet bog and scrub and must have been a miserable ordeal. Nevertheless, they eventually managed to board the *Duquesa* and were joined by survivors of another vessel, probably the tender *Santiago*, which had been wrecked near Inver, Broadhaven Bay, on or about the same day as the *Rata*. Sir Richard Bingham was aware that this large body of Spaniards was in the vicinity but could not be sure of their motives. He was therefore very relieved when the ship set sail, with perhaps 1,000 men (accounts vary) crowded on board. They intended to reach Scotland, as there was little hope of their surviving a voyage to Spain.

Salamander pendant, gold and rubies, from the *Girona* (courtesy of the National Museums Northern Ireland Ulster Museum Collection).

As soon as they reached the open sea they experienced repeatedly shifting winds, which lasted two days, and when a great storm arose on 26 September they anchored in Loughros Mor Bay in south-west County Donegal. The only anchor failed to hold, however, and the *Duquesa* was driven aground near Rosbeg. De Leyva received a bad leg injury as he escaped from the ship and was carried ashore, while his men made for the beach bringing whatever arms, valuables and money they could carry. They camped nearby for eight or nine days and were welcomed by the local chieftain McSweeney, who provided them with food and advice, including the news that another Armada ship, the galleass *Girona*, was anchored in the safe harbour of Killybegs, twenty miles to the south. This was another lifeline for de Leyva and, carried at the head of his little army, he led them across the mountains, which must have been another terrible ordeal. The *Girona* was one of the four galleasses of the Neapolitan squadron and was a cross between a galley and a galleon, with eighteen oars on each side in addition to her sails. She had been involved in many of the English Channel battles and was in poor condition, with a damaged rudder. She had to be made seaworthy before she could set out again, and timber from two small Armada vessels wrecked nearby was used in her repair.

It is not clear how many were on board when she left Killybegs on 26 October but a figure of about 1,300 seems likely. Three hundred had to be left behind, and 40 of these were reported to have been murdered later by the McSweeneys. The fate of the remainder is unknown, but it is unlikely that many survived the wrath of the lord deputy. The plan was to go to Scotland, a distance of about 200 miles, and at first they made reasonably good progress, with the wind directly astern. They passed near Tory Island on the first night, and the following day made further progress along the north coast of Donegal. On 28 October their luck ran out, however, when the wind changed to a northerly direction and they lost control of their rudder. The *Girona* drifted helplessly towards the coast in a strong gale, and that night struck a reef at Lacada Point near the Giant's Causeway in County Antrim. The end came swiftly, and in less than an hour the ship was completely destroyed. The gallant Don Alonso did not survive his third shipwreck in six weeks and drowned alongside the captains of three ships and gentlemen from many of the noblest families in Spain. Only five men got safely ashore. All Spain went into mourning for de Leyva, and it was said that King Philip minded his loss more bitterly than that of all the rest of the fleet.

Other disasters took place further south but none on this scale. Off County Galway on or about 25 September the *Falco Blanco Medina*, a tender, was wrecked off Frenghillaun Island at the entrance to Ballynakill Harbour. All who came ashore were captured and imprisoned in Galway. At the same time the *Concepcion Delcano* of the

King Philip II of Spain.

Biscayan Squadron, with about 200 men, was wrecked on the rocks near Ards, four miles west of Carna in the same county. Those who survived joined their countrymen in Galway jail. Another Armada ship, which has never been identified, anchored off Barna, not far from Galway city, and sent a party of 70 men ashore seeking food and water. They were met by English soldiers from the Galway garrison and forced to surrender. It is believed that a fourth ship was wrecked off Carna but this has never been confirmed. There were now up to 350 prisoners in Galway, of whom 50 or so were spared for ransom. The remainder were executed on Fort Hill, under the supervision of Sir Richard Bingham, with the citizens of the city in attendance. When news reached Dublin that so many prisoners had been spared, the lord deputy was furious that his orders had not been strictly carried out, and the remainder, with two exceptions, were put to death. Those spared were Don Luis de Cordoba, who came from a wealthy and notable Spanish family, and his nephew. Both were eventually ransomed and returned to Spain, and it is reasonable to assume that either Bingham or Fitzwilliam, or both, profited as a result.

The same gale that wrecked the *Concepcion Delcano* forced a huge vessel from the same squadron, the *Gran Grin*, on to the rocky southern shore of Clare Island at the mouth of Clew Bay on the coast of County Mayo. Of the 300 or so men on board, about 100—including Don Pedro de Mendoza, a senior Armada commander— struggled ashore. The island was, as now, the home of the O'Malley clan, whose famous chieftain Grace 'Granuaile' O'Malley was away at the time. The acting chieftain, Dowdarra Roe O'Malley, took the Spaniards prisoner and some weeks later they endeavoured to escape in the clan boats. They were intercepted by the O'Malleys, who killed 68 of them, including Mendoza. Some of those recaptured may have been handed over to Bingham for execution; the fate of the remainder is unknown.

The coast of County Clare claimed three more ships. The *Annunciada*, a converted merchantman built in Ragusa (present-day Dubrovnik), sought safety in the mouth of the River Shannon but was leaking so badly that she was abandoned off Slattery Island on 20 September and set on fire. Her entire complement was transferred to other ships, which eventually reached Spain. The *San Marcos*, a powerful galleon in the Portuguese squadron under the direct command of Medina Sidonia, struck a reef close to Mutton Island near Quilty on the same day and was wrecked. The gales at the time must have been exceptionally severe, as there were only a few survivors out of the estimated 450 on board. Further south, at about the same time, the *San Esteban*, an armed merchantman from northern Spain, ran aground on the White Strand close to Doonbeg and was pounded to pieces by the waves. About 60 out of a total complement of 250 reached the shore alive and were taken prisoner by the English. All were executed by hanging on a hill outside what is now Spanish Point, close to Miltown Malbay, and were buried in a communal grave. Off the coast of County Kerry the weather conditions on 21 September were equally bad, with 'a wind from the west which blew with terrible violence', according to a Spanish source. On that day the galleon *Santa Maria de la Rosa*, vice-flagship of the Guipuzcoa squadron, sought shelter in the Blasket Sound between the Great Blasket Island and the mainland. She was no longer seaworthy and her sails were torn to shreds when she hit a reef and sank almost immediately. Only one man, the son of the ship's pilot, out of a complement of about 500 made it to the shore alive. During his interrogation by the English he told them that the principal officer on the ship was Prince D'Ascoli, a bastard son of Philip II, but this has never been proven. No mercy was shown to this unfortunate boy, who was eventually hanged. Two galleons were already sheltering in the sound and witnessed the sinking but were unable to do anything to help their compatriots. Both had the same name, *San Juan Bautista*, and were from the Portuguese and Castilian squadrons, the former commanded by Don Juan Martinez de Recalde, vice-admiral of the Armada and one of Spain's greatest seamen. Later the same day a Castilian merchantman, by an extraordinary coincidence also named *San Juan Bautista*, struggled into the sound, her mainmast gone, foresail blown to shreds and so battered that her captain had given up all hope of reaching Spain. The following day, when the storm subsided, her crew and soldiers were taken off and transferred to the two galleons. It is not certain what happened to the abandoned ship but it was probably set on fire to avoid capture by the English, the usual Spanish action in such circumstances. With considerable skill, and probably a good bit of luck, both galleons eventually escaped from the sound and reached Corunna ten days later. Recalde, who had been in the forefront of every battle and has been described as 'the greatest hero of the campaign on either side', died four days after reaching home, worn out by sickness, exhaustion and the shame of failure.

Following the sinking of the *Girona* at the end of October, no more hostile ships were seen off the Irish coast, and Sir Richard Bingham was able to inform the lord deputy that 'the Spaniards had departed, leaving but a few sick men'. The threat to English rule was over. No one can be certain how many Armada ships were lost in Irish waters but experts agree that the figure is at least 26. It is also impossible to state the exact loss of life but a figure of 5,250 is considered reasonably accurate, of whom 3,750 were drowned or killed by shipwreck and 1,500 killed or executed by the English or murdered by the Irish. Some 750 are believed to have survived and returned to Spain via Ulster and Scotland. The tragic events of September and

Kinnagoe Bay, Co. Donegal, where the *La Trinidad Valencera* sank. She struck a reef to the left of the rocks in the foreground.

Streedagh Strand, Co. Sligo, where three Armada vessels were pounded to destruction at the same time by violent seas in late September 1588.

White Strand, Great Blasket Island, Co. Kerry, off which two Spanish ships found refuge prior to returning home.

Blasket Sound, Co. Kerry, which the *Santa Maria de la Rosa* entered from the left before striking a reef and sinking immediately.

October 1588 are among the most remarkable in Irish history, and the losses incurred greatly exceed any other naval disaster in Irish coastal waters.

The total loss of ships suffered by the Armada is not known for certain, but at least 60 failed to return to Spain and many of those that did were so badly damaged that they were broken up. Among the first to reach home was Medina Sidonia in his flagship *San Martín*. Soon after his arrival he wrote to the king that

> 'The troubles and miseries we have suffered cannot be described to Your Majesty. They have been worse than have ever been seen in any voyage before. On my own ship, a hundred and eighty men have died of sickness and all the rest of the people on board are ill, many of typhus and other infectious diseases. God be praised for all he has ordained.'

No one knows what the king thought of the humiliating defeat of his 'most felicitous Armada' or the agonies suffered by his soldiers and sailors. We do know, however, that he ordered the clergy and other devout persons to continue, in their private prayers, to commend all his actions to God. Medina Sidonia was only 37 and in the prime of life when he left Lisbon. After four and a half months on board ship, with each day more stressful than the last, he returned home white-haired and a broken man. He never went to sea again.

The defeat of the Armada did not mean the end of Spain's military dominance but marked the beginning of a gradual decline, which culminated in the Treaty of the Pyrenees in 1659, when she lost to France her position as the leading European power.

2

THE *ROCHDALE* AND THE *PRINCE OF WALES*

For the citizens of Dublin, the weather during November 1807 was the coldest in living memory for that time of the year. Snow lay thickly in the city and countryside, and local charities appealed for ever more generous contributions to alleviate the suffering of the numerous poor and destitute. Napoleon was at the height of his power and there was little prospect of an early end to the war with France in which Ireland, as part of the United Kingdom, was actively involved. As if these woes were not enough, the worst-ever shipping disaster on the southern coastline of Dublin Bay was about to unfold.

On the afternoon of Wednesday 18 November the brig *Rochdale* and the sloop *Prince of Wales* sailed from the Pidgeon House, Ringsend, in a convoy of five ships bound for Liverpool. The great majority of the passengers were army officers, non-commissioned officers and soldiers with their wives and families, including men from the Cork and Mayo militias. The latter were being transferred to the 18th Royal Irish and 97th Queen's German Regiments to augment the huge number of Irishmen already serving in the regular British Army at that time.

As the ships left port they were met by an easterly gale, and when darkness fell this increased to storm force. The following morning they were seen in obvious trouble at the entrance to Dublin Bay as they endeavoured to regain the safety of the port. The wind then came round to east-south-east and strengthened further, while squalls of snow and sleet hid them from the sight of those on shore. Later that day the *Rochdale*, under the command of Captain Hodgson, was seen under bare poles off Dalkey, where she tried to anchor without success. Showing blue lights and with men firing muskets to attract attention, she drove past the pier of the small harbour at Dunleary before crashing ashore with great force at Seapoint, just below where the Martello tower, built only a few years previously, now stands. Her hull was staved in and all 265 persons said to be on board perished. It has been suggested that the reason nobody survived is that heavy snow so limited visibility that those on board were

Shipping at the entrance to Dublin port in the early nineteenth century, by William Sadler (1782–1839) (courtesy of Adam's, Dublin).

A brig under full sail.

unaware that they were so close to land. A letter to the editor of the *Freeman's Journal* a few days later criticised the failure of any lifeboat to come to their rescue.

The *Prince of Wales* fared no better. Early the same day her master, Robert Jones, tried to reach Howth, but the wind, which he described as a hurricane, blew with such force that he lost his sails and was driven towards Bray Head, where he threw out all his anchors but they did not hold. Instead his ship was dragged along the coast past Dalkey, Dunleary and Seapoint, until that evening, in the dark, it struck the beach about 200 yards from the shore at Black Rock, then the only town of any size between Dublin city and Dunleary. Jones managed to release the longboat and, together with the ship's steward, his wife and son, two soldiers and the rest of the crew, made it safely to the shore. There were no other survivors and the ship was battered to pieces on the strand. One hundred and twenty people lost their lives, almost all soldiers, and no attempt was made to rescue them, the weather being described as 'too tempestuous'.

An inquest was held on 27 November, at which one of the only two passengers saved—South Mayo militiaman Anthony McIntyre—accused Jones and his men of pulling up the ladders that led to the hold, thus preventing those below from coming on deck. It was also claimed that the hatchways had been nailed down, but following an examination of the wreck this was found to be untrue. The first charge stood, however, and Jones and most of his crew were held in Newgate prison to face trial on a charge of murder. Proceedings were eventually dropped, probably because of insufficient evidence, but we know that Jones was quoted as saying that he didn't care who died as long as his crew was safe and the accusation rings true.

The full extent of the loss of life became clear when the storm abated. Dead men, women and children were scattered all along the strand and in amongst the rocks between Dunleary and Black Rock. The *Freeman's Journal* reported that there was a scene of indescribable horror at Seapoint, just below the house owned by Sir Thomas Lees. Over the taffrail of the *Rochdale* a woman's corpse hung by a broken leg, while all around lay terribly mutilated bodies. Empty trunks, masts, sails, casks, mattresses, clothes and provisions of every kind were strewn along the coast. Over the following days the dead were removed to makeshift morgues and buried in Carrickbrennan and Merrion graveyards, where memorials can still be seen. The same newspaper reported that, despite soldiers being on patrol along the coast, many items had been looted from the wrecked ships by gangs from Dunleary and Ringsend, and a reward of twenty guineas was offered for information leading to their arrest. Six men were eventually convicted and sent to Kilmainham jail.

For centuries prior to these sinkings there had been continuous deaths from

Martello tower, Seapoint, Co. Dublin. The *Rochdale* was wrecked on the rocks to the right.

shipwrecks in Dublin Bay, but never so many people lost at the same time. Seasoned sailors described the port of Dublin as the most perilous in the world for a ship to leave or approach when caught in an east-north-easterly or south-south-easterly gale. Following this disaster, public opinion demanded that a cure be found for the ever-growing list of deaths in the bay and various suggestions were made, the most improbable being a canal between Sandycove and Dublin city. Eventually, after unrelenting pressure on the authorities in London, it was agreed that a harbour of refuge should be built, incorporating the little fishing port at Dunleary, which in those days was surrounded by an uninhabited inhospitable wasteland. The foundation stone was laid in 1817 by the lord lieutenant, and it was completed five years later to give us the splendid harbour we know today at Dun Laoghaire (originally Kingstown), with its two massive granite piers enclosing 250 acres of water. It is certainly one of the most charming and picturesque artificial harbours in the world, has saved many lives and has been of great benefit to Irish shipping.

3

THE *QUEEN VICTORIA* AND THE MISSING FOG-BELL

Dublin Bay and its approaches have seen a greater concentration of sinkings than anywhere else in Ireland, which is not surprising as it has always been the principal gateway to the country from the time Vikings settled in what is now Dublin city in the ninth century. Since then countless vessels of every type have plied their trade in its waters. Until the middle of the nineteenth century it was a hazardous place for shipping, and close on 1,500 shipwrecks have been officially confirmed in the coastal waters of County Dublin; the full total will never be known.

As commerce and communication between Ireland and England and Wales increased, a mail-packet service became necessary and was established as far back as 1572 between Ringsend at the mouth of the River Liffey and Liverpool. By 1768 there were also six sailings a week to Holyhead. In the early nineteenth century the mail-boat sailed from Howth, but Kingstown became its final port in 1826.

The paddle-steamer *Queen Victoria*, built in Liverpool in 1837 and owned by the City of Dublin Steam Packet Company, at one time carried the mail from Kingstown to Liverpool. Capable of eleven knots and 150ft long, she later carried passengers and cargo between Ireland and Great Britain on a regular basis. Her safety provisions were reputed to be particularly good for the time and included an extra lifeboat and 90 cork lifejackets. Her skipper, Captain Church, was described as an officer of great experience, high in the confidence of his employers and upwards of twenty years in the service.

On the afternoon of 14 February 1853 the *Queen Victoria* left Liverpool *en route* for Dublin with a crew of 25 and 99 passengers, twelve of whom had cabins. The weather was fine, the wind north-north-east and it continued like this until early next morning, when light snow began to fall as they neared the Irish coast. At this stage the Kish light on the southern approach to Dublin Bay and the Baily lighthouse on Howth Head could be clearly seen. Gradually the snow came down very heavily and visibility was greatly reduced, but the ship seems to have maintained its speed and those on board assumed that they were sailing clear into Dublin Bay. Suddenly, the

A view of the Baily lighthouse and shipping in Dublin Bay in the nineteenth century by E. Hayes (courtesy of Adam's, Dublin).

first mate saw cliffs looming straight ahead and immediately gave orders to stop the engines, but it was too late and she crashed headlong upon rocks close to the shore just a little north of the Baily lighthouse.

Almost immediately about twelve of the passengers and crew scrambled over her bows, eight of whom succeeded in obtaining a footing on the rocks. From there they reached higher ground, where they were later discovered in a deplorable condition from exhaustion and exposure. Cabin passengers rushed half-naked up to the snowy deck, where they joined the steerage passengers running around in wild confusion. Captain Church endeavoured to calm them but without success and, thinking that the vessel was still seaworthy, gave orders to reverse the engines, with the apparent intention of running her ashore on the North Bull Island. As soon as they reached deep water, however, she began to sink. The deck was now crowded with passengers, screaming, praying and crying for help. As cries for assistance became louder and louder, there was a general rush towards the ship's boats. The one on the starboard quarter was immediately filled but slipped from her davit into the sea, where she was instantly swamped and all on board perished.

The boat on the port side was successfully launched but soon began to sink, until it was discovered that the plug-hole was open. A young lad immediately thrust his fingers into it and partially checked the leak while the water was bailed out. Two of those on board, Charles Ralph, a Wicklow shipowner, and William Kegg of the Royal Navy, took control and rowed towards the rocks, where they safely landed fourteen people. They then rowed over to the steamer *Roscommon*, which had just reached the scene, and obtained a plug for the hole, after which they returned to find that the *Queen Victoria* had sunk, with only her masts, funnel and spars above water. They rescued another six people who were clinging to these remnants and brought them to safety. By this time the *Roscommon* had launched her boats and she is credited with saving the lives of about 40 people. Had she not been in the vicinity the loss of life would have been far greater.

The steamer *Iron Duke* and a pilot boat were dispatched from Kingstown to aid in the rescue but did not reach Howth Head until midday, by which time there was no hope of anyone surviving in the harsh winter conditions. They managed to find four dead bodies but many others had been carried away by the strong current or were entombed within the wreck. These included Captain Church and his second mate, both of whom went down with their ship. By a sad coincidence the third mate of the *Iron Duke* was Church's son. No one knows for certain how many died on that fateful night but a total of about 60 would appear to be correct.

An official government enquiry was held two days later in the boardroom of the

The wrecking of the *Queen Victoria* at the Baily lighthouse (courtesy of the National Maritime Museum, Greenwich, London).

Kingstown Police Office and continued the following week. Its findings were that the captain and first mate had been negligent in not having a lookout in the bow and failing to slow the ship or take soundings when visibility was so poor owing to the heavy snow. Had these measures been carried out, it was felt, the tragedy would never have happened. There was further criticism of Captain Church for his hastiness in reversing the engines after the *Queen Victoria* struck; there was evidence to suggest that he panicked and did not check the extent of the damage caused by the collision before making his decision. Many of the witnesses felt that most of those on board would have survived had the vessel remained on the rocks. Nevertheless, the greatest criticism was reserved for the Board of the Ballast Office for failing to place a fog-bell on the Howth promontory.

A leading article in the *Freeman's Journal* accused the Board of culpable and criminal negligence. It drew attention to the fact that seven years previously during a dense fog the steamer *Prince*, with the Liberator, Daniel O'Connell, on board, had struck the rocks at the very point where the *Queen Victoria* went down and had narrowly escaped being wrecked. Subsequently, great efforts were made to force the Board to erect an effective fog-bell in the area, but despite promises and O'Connell's private urgings nothing was done. All parties at the enquiry agreed that had a fog-bell been in place it was very unlikely the accident would have occurred.

The non-appearance of the local lifeboats does not appear to have been questioned, which is remarkable bearing in mind the criticism heaped on the Board of the Ballast Office for their failure to install the fog-bell. There are two possible explanations. Firstly, the only stations in Dublin Bay in 1853 were Kingstown and Poolbeg, and Nicholas Leach in his excellent book *The Lifeboat Service in Ireland* suggests that they were in a rundown state at the time owing to a lack of funding, with boats in a poor state of repair and inadequate for the job. Secondly, there is the possibility that neither was aware of the unfolding disaster, bearing in mind that communications were so poor in those days. Even so, it is surprising that when the *Iron Duke* was dispatched from Kingstown it was not accompanied by the lifeboat, unless the pilot boat fulfilled that role. There was also a lifeboat at nearby Howth, but it does not appear to have been launched either.

THE EMIGRANT SHIP *TAYLEUR*

The discovery of gold in the British colonies of Victoria and New South Wales in 1851 resulted in a substantial increase in the number of people seeking a new life in Australia. Between 1852 and 1857 nearly a quarter of a million immigrants arrived from the British Isles, and during 1854 over 40,000 of these sailed from Liverpool in 107 ships. This was a bonanza for the shipping companies, who were already making huge profits, and there was a constant demand for new, bigger and faster vessels.

The *Tayleur* was designed to meet these requirements. Named after her owner, Charles Tayleur, whose likeness was carved as a figurehead on her bowsprit, she had an iron hull, iron masts, three decks, spacious saloons, private cabins and berths for 400 passengers. Advertised as 'this magnificent new clipper-ship which will undoubtedly prove to be the fastest of the Australian fleet', she was, in fact, the largest iron sailing-ship in Europe up to that time.

Built at Warrington, an inland town on the River Mersey, she was launched on 5 October 1853 and towed to Liverpool by three steam tugs. There she was fitted up and prepared for her maiden voyage to Melbourne under Captain John Noble, an experienced seaman who had commanded ships on voyages to Australia, America and China. There was great demand for accommodation, and 650 people, the great majority described as 'a superior class of emigrant', came on board. There was also general cargo valued at £20,000. Government agents examined the health of the passengers and found everything satisfactory; everyone seemed assured of a successful and pleasant voyage.

There were, however, certain flaws not obvious at the time. First, there is no evidence that the ship or crew underwent any form of sea trials prior to departure, nor were the compasses properly checked, which was of great importance where iron-hulled ships were concerned. Second, there was difficulty in forming a crew. Eventually 70 were taken on, some of whom had little knowledge of the English language; only 26 were able seamen.

The *Tayleur* (courtesy of the National Library of Ireland).

There was much cheering and general excitement on board when the steam tug *Victory* towed the *Tayleur* down the Mersey and out to sea at noon on Thursday 19 January 1854. By 8pm she reached Holyhead, where the pilot disembarked, and then headed down the Irish Sea in increasingly bad weather. Soon a strong south-westerly gale was blowing and the captain was forced to beat about. The gale continued the following day, forcing the ship northward and making life difficult for the crew, who had to be assisted by those passengers with some knowledge of nautical affairs.

Early on Saturday morning they were still close to where the pilot had left the ship 30 hours previously, but in improving weather and under full sail made good progress. By 11am, in thick and hazy conditions and with a high sea running, Captain Noble supposed their position to be twenty miles or so east of Wicklow Head. An hour or so later the weather cleared a little and land was sighted about a mile dead ahead. Frantic efforts were made to alter course but to no avail, following which both anchors were let go in an effort to slow the ship. Both 'snapped like a carrot', according to one survivor, and the *Tayleur*, now completely out of control, struck broadside against a ridge of rocks adjoining the cliffs on the north-east of Lambay Island, three miles from the north County Dublin coast, near a promontory known as 'the Nose' in what is now Tayleur Bay.

There are diverse descriptions by survivors of what happened next. All are agreed that the decks were swarming with passengers when the ship struck with great force, causing utter confusion on board. Fortunately, the forecastle on the starboard side was so close to the ledge that it was possible for some men to jump ashore. Planks and spars were then made fast to the shore and it was by means of this makeshift bridge that the majority of the survivors reached safety. Others were saved by swinging hand over hand across a number of ropes secured between the rigging and rock outcrops. Suddenly, the *Tayleur* heeled over towards the sea, filled rapidly and went down stern foremost. As it sank, scores of people were washed overboard and either drowned or were battered to death against the cliffs. Captain Noble was the last man to leave the ship as the hull slipped below the water. He swam towards the rocks and by means of a rope thrown to him was hauled to safety. Two men sought refuge in the rigging of a mast still above water, and one was rescued by the coastguard when they arrived at the scene. They were unable to reach the other but upon returning the next morning succeeded in rescuing him also. He had been exposed to the elements for fourteen hours.

One can only imagine the state of mind of the survivors when they suddenly found themselves stranded on an unknown shore in the middle of winter. Drenched to the skin, in many cases half-naked, horrified by what they had experienced and with their belongings at the bottom of the sea, they must have been a pitiful sight. Darkness would have fallen about 4pm. Some found their way to the houses of the islanders, who numbered about 80, mainly tenant farmers. Others reached the coastguard station or the castle owned by the local landlord, Lord Talbot de Malahide. It seems very likely that some spent a wretched night in the open. Fortunately, one of the passengers, Robert Kemp, with three others managed to get to the mainland in a scallop boat and reported the wreck to Sir Roger Palmer of Kenure House, Rush, who immediately dispatched fourteen gallons of whiskey, three sheep, potatoes and oatmeal to the island.

At 10am next day, a Sunday, Kemp met John Walsh, Lloyd's agent in Dublin, and the latter immediately and at his own expense chartered the steamer *Prince*, loaded it with provisions and sailed to Lambay, where they anchored that night after a stormy passage. Early on Monday morning the survivors, excluding Captain Noble and 25 of the crew, were ferried on board and brought to Dublin, where they were supplied with cash donated by local merchants and lodged in comfortable accommodation. Remarkably, only four were seriously injured and they were brought to Jervis Street hospital, where they made a good recovery. On Tuesday 24 January the survivors again boarded the *Prince* and sailed to Liverpool, the entire cost being met by the City of Dublin Steam Packet Company. The exact number who survived, including the crew, is not absolutely clear but the official figure was 290. The following month, 88 of these

The *Tayleur* on the rocks at Lambay (courtesy of the National Library of Ireland).

sailed for Australia on the *Golden Era* and reached Melbourne safely five months later.

Meanwhile, on Lambay Island the coastguard and Captain Noble and his men had the unenviable task of recovering as many bodies as possible. Owing to bad weather they were unable to use a boat for this purpose, so a derrick was erected on the cliffs. It was then necessary for a man to be lowered to attach the bodies to a rope—dangerous work in the conditions. A week later only 100 or so bodies had been recovered, many so mutilated that they were impossible to identify. The great majority were buried in unmarked graves in the cemetery attached to the old church on the island, and some others on the mainland at St Andrew's Church of Ireland church in Malahide. The sea claimed the remainder. A total of 360 people had died, of whom over 100 were women. Only three females were saved, along with a single child, who died ten weeks later. By contrast, only six of the crew perished.

An inquest was held at Davis's Hotel (now the Grand Hotel), Malahide, Co. Dublin, towards the end of January 1854 and lasted three days. There was evidence that the ship was undermanned and that some of the crew could not understand English. They had no opportunity prior to the voyage to get to know one another. There was also criticism that this newly launched ship did not undergo sea trials prior to departure. It was suggested that there might have been a design fault in the rudder. The verdict finally delivered by the jury was

View of Tayleur Bay by Paul Kelly (courtesy of the Gorry Gallery, Dublin).

'that this deplorable accident occurred in consequence of the highly culpable neglect of the owners in permitting the vessel to leave port without her compasses being properly adjusted, or a sufficient trial having taken place to learn whether she was under the control of her helm or not. And we find that Captain Noble did not take sufficient precautions to ensure the safety of the vessel by sounding after he found the compasses were in error; but we consider that from the time the vessel came in sight of land he acted with coolness and courage and every exertion in his power to save all the lives of the passengers not having left the ship until she was completely under water.'

The Liverpool Marine Board met on 5 April 1854 to consider Captain Noble's future and two days later announced, *inter alia*, 'that he is, neither from incompetence nor from any other cause, unfit to discharge the duties of a master and this board recommend the renewal of his certificate of competency'. There was one other factor that, surprisingly, was not mentioned during either enquiry: the day before the *Tayleur* was launched, Noble had fallen 25ft into the hold of the ship and was badly shaken but otherwise apparently uninjured. In light of this it seems reasonable to suggest that he was not fully fit when he went to sea and that his judgement may have been impaired, with disastrous results. We shall never know.

A charity known as the 'Tayleur Fund' was set up and administered by many of Dublin's leading merchants to assist the survivors by way of cash, clothing, accommodation and free passage home. Long afterwards, the fund continued to help seamen whose ship had been wrecked and only ceased in 1913, when the remaining £1,500 was used for the provision of a petrol-engined lifeboat for the Royal National Lifeboat Institution. The fund also awarded medals to people who performed acts of gallantry or behaved beyond the call of duty when maritime disasters arose in the Irish Sea. John Walsh, the Lloyd's agent who had given such great assistance to the victims of the *Tayleur*, was an early recipient of their gold medal.

There are striking similarities between the *Tayleur* and the *Titanic* in 1912. Both were state-of-the-art ships in the 'White Star' fleet, being larger, faster, more strongly built and more comfortable than most of their contemporaries. They were lavishly praised by their owners, especially from the safety aspect, and public interest was intense. Both sank on their maiden voyage with great loss of life. The *Titanic* hit an iceberg head-on; the *Tayleur* struck a cliff in a similar manner. All of the passengers on the *Tayleur* were emigrating to a far-distant land, as were over 500 of those on the *Titanic*. Both are notable examples of pride going before a fall.

Her Majesty's gunboat *Wasp*

Tory Island, seven miles from the nearest point on the mainland of County Donegal, is the most remote of the inhabited Irish islands. The north-eastern side has fine cliff scenery, but the western end is very flat and fringed with dangerous rocks, on which there have been many wrecks. A lighthouse, 122 feet above high water, was erected close to this coast in 1832.

Many British warships were lost in the vicinity of Tory during the First and Second World Wars, the most significant being the sinking of HMS *Audacious* off Malin Head on 27 October 1914. This powerful, state-of-the-art battleship was considered unsinkable, but the pride of the Royal Navy blew up and disappeared twelve hours after it was fatally damaged by a German mine. All on board were saved but the loss was kept a secret throughout the war, during which it remained on the Navy List.

During the Second World War the liner *Queen Mary* was used to convey United States servicemen from America to ports in Great Britain. She relied on her great speed to avoid German U-boats in the mid-Atlantic, but as she approached the Irish coast and the danger increased an escort was provided. On 1 October 1942 and bound for Scotland with 10,000 Americans on board, she was joined by an old Great War cruiser, HMS *Curacao*, for the final leg of the voyage. As an additional means of defence the *Queen Mary* made frequent alterations in course, and while engaged in such a manoeuvre on 2 October off the north-west coast of Tory she collided with the cruiser, which apparently tried to pass in front of her, and sliced her in two with such force that she immediately sank and over 300 sailors lost their lives. The liner's bow was badly damaged but she managed to make port safely. At the subsequent court martial the captains of both ships were found to be negligent for not keeping a proper lookout.

The worst shipping tragedy to affect Tory Island directly was the sinking of Her Majesty's vessel *Wasp* under the lighthouse early on the morning of Monday 22

Her Majesty's gunboat *Wasp* (courtesy of the National Library of Ireland).

September 1884. The *Wasp* was a composite gunboat of 455 tons and 145ft in length, with a light draught, capable of running close ashore and up rivers. Commissioned at Devonport in 1881, she mounted four guns and two machine-guns and was powered by steam and schooner-rigged sails. She had a crew of about 50, and four boats swung from the davits.

Since 1883 the *Wasp* had been based in Queenstown (Cobh) and operated along the southern and western coasts of Ireland. For much of 1884 she was on special service on the north-west coast, bringing commissioners of the Harbour Fishery Board around different harbours and rivers where information and statistics relevant to fishing and navigation were being collected. She was also hired by the Society of Friends (Quakers) to supply food and assistance on their behalf to starving people in County Donegal and elsewhere. Many of the crew had close contact with these unfortunates, including the surgeon, who did what he could for the sick and dying. Other work included fishery protection and the prevention of smuggling. A most unpopular duty was that of bringing sheriffs, soldiers and police to the offshore islands for the purpose of rent enforcement and evictions. These were activities that the navy hated.

At 6am on the morning of 21 September 1884 the *Wasp* left Westport in County Mayo on such a mission. Their orders were to sail to Moville in Lough Foyle, where they were to take on board an eviction party and then proceed to the tiny island of Inishtrahull off Malin Head, where several families were to be thrown out of their hovels. From the outset their journey of nearly 250 miles was unusual, because it was to be completed in one leg and involved sailing by night; normally gunboats only travelled by day and sought the sanctuary of a safe harbour each nightfall.

Under steam the gunboat made good progress at first and reached Rathlin-Obeirnie Island near Glencolumbkille in the early afternoon, at which stage orders were given to turn off the engine and proceed under sail. This reduced her speed considerably, and Arranmore Island was not reached until 10pm. From there the shortest route to Moville would have been via Tory Sound, the channel between Tory and the mainland, but this is a dangerous passage, especially at night, and, still under sail, a course was set to go around the island. It was now dark and cloudy, with a strong north-westerly wind and squally showers, but the light on Tory became visible about 2am on Monday morning and sometime later could be seen off the port bow. At this stage Lieutenant George King (first officer and navigator), who was on watch, roused his captain, Lieutenant Commander John Nicholls, for permission to change course but his request was refused. It appears that a dispute arose between them, but Nicholls was adamant that his orders should be obeyed and the course remained the same. Some time later the light was seen dead ahead, and just before 4am the gunboat ran upon an isolated rock known as 'An Feadan' and broke her back. There was pandemonium on board as she began to fill rapidly and orders were given to lower the boats, but it was too late and they were dashed against the reef. It is estimated that only fifteen minutes elapsed from the time the ship struck until she sank in twenty fathoms of water. In that time the crew struggled to break free and reach the shore, but only six managed to do so. Although they were only 40 yards or so from the lighthouse, it was daylight before the light-keeper realised that a tragedy had taken place and came to the assistance of the survivors, some of whom were found unconscious. Fifty-one of those on board, including all the officers, died and many of the bodies were never recovered.

This was a disaster that should never have happened, and in its aftermath questions were asked which have never been satisfactorily answered. Why, having reached Rathlin-Obeirnie Island in good time, were the engines shut down? Why

The *Wasp* on the rocks below the lighthouse on Tory Island (courtesy of the National Library of Ireland).

was it decided to sail around one of the most dangerous coasts in Ireland at night? Why was the engine not reactivated to ensure that Tory was weathered safely when a strong north-westerly wind was blowing and they were on a lee shore? Why were they so far off course as they approached the island? All of these failures suggest poor seamanship, careless navigation and woeful decision-making on the part of Lieutenant Commander Nicholls, but this seems entirely out of character.

Newspaper reports following the sinking describe the 45-year-old Scot as a most skilful sailor with a good reputation who took great pride in his ship, the remarkably neat trim of which always evoked favourable comments. A letter from the Society of Friends praised his interest in the welfare of his crew and the skill he displayed in the navigation of his vessel. The Piers and Harbours Commissioners expressed their great regret on hearing of his death and recollected the care and skill with which the vessel was navigated whenever they came on board. They also emphasised that the captain knew Tory well, having been there five or six times, and could not account for his failure on this occasion. Mention was also made of his courtesy and good nature and the many friends he had made on the Irish coast. Was this the same man who sailed from Moville that September? Had he become unwell or depressed and incapable of command? We shall never know, but it seems reasonable to suggest that something of the sort occurred.

It is evident that the *Wasp* was badly handled that fateful night, and if the captain was unable to take proper command the response of the first officer would have been all-important. The 24-year-old Lieutenant King had only been on board for a few weeks, however, and this was his first ship. It was also the first time that he had been on the north-west coast of Ireland, and if, as navigator and officer of the watch, he found that he was on a wrong course and heading for an unfamiliar island in treacherous seas, what was he to do if his captain insisted that no evasive action was necessary? To disobey his senior officer would have meant a court martial and almost certain dismissal from the service. It is, of course, pure conjecture, but in such a stressful situation he would probably be incapable of making the right decision until it was too late. After a court martial in Portsmouth on 10 October 1884, the lords of the Admiralty decided 'that the cause of the loss must be attributed to want of care and attention in the navigation of the gunboat'—a fairly bland statement in the circumstances.

Poor morale on the part of the crew may also have been a factor, however. A month or so previously, a party of sailors went ashore on Clare Island, where there were very unpleasant scenes during evictions. The prospect of being involved in such activities again would have been most unwelcome. In this connection, an article dated 25 September 1884 from the County Donegal correspondent of the *Freeman's Journal* is of interest. He writes, *inter alia*, as follows:

> 'The sadness of this disaster is heightened by the duty which the officers and crew
> of the *Wasp* were about to enter upon. I could not feel my conscience free if I did
> not expose, shall I say the iniquity of the eviction work that they would be assisting
> in before the setting of the sun that Monday evening. The island of Inishtrahull lies
> about ten miles north-west of Malin Head. Its population consists of less than
> twenty families. The surface is almost entirely rock with miserable little patches of
> sandy soil amongst the boulders. Like several of the islands of the seaboard of
> Donegal it does not yield any fuel. The rigours of the winter make it almost
> uninhabitable. The residents preserve their existence chiefly by fishing. This is the
> place and those were the people to which the *Wasp* was to have conveyed an armed
> force of Police and the agents of Law for the casting out of several families from
> their miserable homes. One's blood almost boils at the thought of these things.
> Surely the time has come when the Naval force of the Empire should not be
> requisitioned for "Particular Duty" of such disgraceful character.'

It is probable that everyone on the gunboat would have agreed with this latter
comment. Some of the officers may have considered evictions necessary and justified
in certain circumstances, but the crew would be on the side of those thrown out of
their homes. Many would have come from a humble background and would have
known what it was like to be poor. As she headed north, the *Wasp* may not have been
a happy ship and discipline on board may have suffered as a result.

The lords of the Admiralty may have been puzzled at the loss of their gunboat
but the natives of Tory knew better: the real cause was the power of the cursing
stones. The islanders have always been a very independent people who at one time
were pirates and constantly raided the mainland. Legends describe their leader, Balor,
god of darkness, as having a single eye in the centre of his forehead, while his glance
was sufficient to kill. It may be from those ancient times that the myth of the flat,
speckled cursing stones situated in the middle of the island arose. They were activated
by the king of Tory (there is still a 'king' today) or his official curser by being turned
anticlockwise three times as an ancient spell was uttered and the object of their
displeasure was named. The last time they are known to have been used was against
the *Wasp*, which had visited on a number of occasions in an effort to collect
outstanding rents. The curser put a spell on the ship, carried out the traditional
procedures and, lo and behold, the gunboat was destroyed. The story adds a certain
piquancy to the mysterious sinking, the exact cause of which we shall never know.

6

THE LAST VOYAGE OF THE *PORT YARROCK*

The *Port Yarrock* was an ironclad three-masted barque, 230ft long with a tonnage of 1,379, built in Glasgow in 1886. By that time many ships had a steam engine in addition to sail but she depended on sail only. She was one of the Port Line ships owned by Crawford and Rowat of Glasgow, who had a reputation for penny-pinching and were thought to set profit above the safety of their seamen.

On 29 October 1892 the *Port Yarrock* set sail from Cardiff on the long journey to Santa Rosalia in the Gulf of California under the command of Captain Thomas Forbes, a Scot, and with a crew of 21. The latter consisted of a first and second mate, carpenter, sail-maker, cook, steward, seven able-bodied seamen, mostly Scandinavian with a limited knowledge of English, and eight boys between the ages of fifteen and nineteen. Six of these boys had never been to sea before and at the outset were useless as seamen.

The ship encountered very bad weather for the greater part of the voyage and took an entire month to battle around Cape Horn. She finally reached Santa Rosalia in the Gulf of California, their first and only port of call, on 19 April 1893, having been at sea for five and a half arduous months. Being at anchor brought no respite to the ship's boys, who were given the dirty and back-breaking job of unloading the cargo of peat briquettes on to lighters in dreadfully hot and unhealthy conditions. This was because the owners, to save money, had instructed the captain not to employ local labour. Later they had to load 1,000 tons of copper ore worth £100,000 (about €5,000,000 today) for the return journey. Captain Forbes and his crew spent 79 days in that small, isolated port, and one wonders how they passed the time when not on duty. We know there was a lot of heavy drinking, which Forbes and his first mate endeavoured to control, especially as their departure date drew near. During all of their stay there was a shortage of clean water and vegetables; many of the crew were unwell and the boys were terribly homesick. One of the able seamen, an Italian, was thrown off the ship when he attacked an officer with a shovel. It is not clear why it

A typical late nineteenth-century barque. This is the *Herzogin Cecilie.*

Kilcummin Strand, near where the *Port Yarrock* was wrecked.

was necessary to stay so long at Santa Rosalia, but the loading of the copper ore would have been a lengthy and difficult job.

They finally set sail for Queenstown on 7 July 1893 but almost immediately were becalmed for two weeks and did not cross the equator until 26 August. Calms and unfavourable winds continued to plague them as they headed south, but they eventually entered the Atlantic on 14 October, after rounding Cape Horn in fine weather. Seven days earlier the steward had committed suicide by shooting himself in the head with a revolver after the captain discovered that he had sold the ship's lime-juice (compulsory on all British sailing-ships to prevent scurvy) and other supplies at Santa Rosalia for his own profit. On 15 November they sighted the islands of Trinidad and Martin Vas, 600 miles east of Brazil, and recrossed the equator on the 29th of the same month.

The *Port Yarrock* was now on course for Queenstown, which the crew hoped would be reached by Christmas. The vessel was not properly manned, however, as most of those on board were undernourished, with some suffering from scurvy. The situation worsened as food supplies ran low and rations were reduced. On Christmas Day they were still at sea in miserable, cold, wet conditions and with little to eat, but were hopeful of reaching port before the end of the year. Instead they encountered terrible storms, and when 1 January 1894 dawned they were off course on the west

Some of the crew in the bow of the *Port Yarrock* on a previous voyage (courtesy of Mrs Heather Cartridge).

coast of Ireland, where they were battered by violent gales for the next two weeks. With the captain and crew in a state of almost complete exhaustion and the sails torn to shreds, it seems little short of a miracle that they eventually found refuge in Brandon Bay, Co. Kerry, on 20 January. A local pilot, Denis Lynch, rowed out to meet them, and the *Port Yarrock* found a temporary anchorage close to the pier at the village of Brandon.

Captain Forbes, who was described locally as extremely stressed and unwell, went ashore and returned with potatoes, some fresh meat and biscuits, but there was little else available in that poor fishing village. Normally there would have been fish, but no boats had gone to sea for four weeks because of the terrible weather. He later visited Lloyd's agent in Tralee, about 30 miles away, who warned him that his ship was in a dangerous place and offered him a choice of two steamers to tow her to a safe harbour. Forbes replied that he would have to contact the owners and sent them telegrams asking for instructions. After a long delay they replied that there was a tug on its way from Liverpool and that the *Port Yarrock* should remain at Brandon until its arrival. We do not know how the crew fared in the meantime except that the village women baked bread for them and did their best to offer support. There is no evidence that they received any kind of medical attention from the shore.

On 26 January, when they had been at Brandon about a week, the Liverpool tug arrived but was unable to arrange the tow, as the weather worsened and she was forced to run in close to the pier for shelter. The following day a fierce gale was blowing, and the *Port Yarrock* began to drag her anchors in the early afternoon and drifted out to sea. The next morning she was seen by watchers all along the coast drifting southwards in a northerly gale, and in the early afternoon ran aground 600 yards from Kilcummin Strand near the village of Stradbally. Blue flares were fired by the stricken vessel and at 7.30 that evening the Fenit lifeboat with a crew of thirteen set out on a rescue mission. Whilst they managed to get across Tralee Bay, the weather again deteriorated and they were forced to anchor in the lee of the Magharee Islands. Next morning (29 January) they made another attempt but were driven back and had to return to Fenit after being at sea for thirteen hours. No other boat capable of coping with the raging seas was available, and those on shore watched helplessly as the *Port Yarrock* gradually disintegrated. One after the other the three masts collapsed as huge waves dashed over her, until she suddenly split in two and sank in the centre, with both ends raised up. Those on shore could hear cries from the crew, but only one man was seen to jump from the wreck in the hope of swimming to safety. About an hour later the bodies of Captain Forbes, the first mate and a Norwegian seaman were washed ashore. Thirteen other bodies, three of them decapitated, were found

Philip Baines, aged eighteen (courtesy of Mrs Heather Cartridge).

later but only one could be identified; there were no survivors.

An inquest on the first three bodies was held in Rohan's Public House, Stradbally, on 2 February. In his summing-up the coroner expressed astonishment at Captain Forbes's repeated refusal to accept help locally and criticised the owners for their failure to reply promptly to telegrams seeking their instructions. He also deplored the lack of a local lifeboat and telegraph office, whose presence would have made the rescue of the crew much more likely. The bodies were then buried in the adjoining graveyard, with many local people in attendance.

We know about the awful hardship of that fourteen-month ordeal because of long letters written to his parents by Philip Baines, a senior apprentice, who was eighteen at the start of the voyage. He was from a comfortable background and his family, including eight brothers and sisters, lived in a fine Georgian house at Escrick, York. Another younger apprentice, John Carnie of Edinburgh, with a similar background, and two other apprentices also wrote letters home, which are still extant and mirror those of Baines. All of these letters have come to light as a result of research by Sheila Mulcahy, who lives in County Kerry, and are described in her book *A gallant barque*.

The loss of the *Port Yarrock* was widely reported in the local and national press, and it is very likely that this is how the next of kin received the news. At about the same time the families of the dead apprentices would have received the letters from their sons posted in Tralee. Their grief, compounded by the grim facts of which they were now aware, must have been heartbreaking. It also made the recipients very angry, and William Baines, Philip's father, wrote immediately to the coroner, telling him what he had learned about the voyage home; unfortunately his letter did not arrive until after the inquest. He also took steps to expose the failings that led to the tragedy by writing to the papers, as did other parents of the apprentices, while questions were asked in the House of Commons over a period of three weeks by prominent members, including a retired admiral. All pressed successfully for a full enquiry by the Board of Trade.

This was held in Glasgow during the last week of March 1894. At least six people travelled from Kerry, including Lloyd's agent W.H. McCowen, the pilot Denis Lynch and Robert Melvin, coxswain of the Fenit lifeboat. A variety of witnesses were questioned on all aspects of the sinking, but the main thrust of the enquiry was the question of undermanning. The court held that the owners—and, in particular, the managing director, Robert J. Rowat—were seriously negligent in this respect and that it was the primary cause of the disaster. This enquiry was widely reported, and a *Times* editorial commented, *inter alia*, that 'seldom has condemnation so severe been passed upon any owner of a British merchant vessel'. It was also pointed out that while the Board of Trade had strict rules about a ship's load line, equipment, stores and everything belonging to her, there were none about the human agents who were to man her. This remarkable loophole was closed three years later when amendments were made to the Merchant Shipping Act 1894, which included undermanning as a reason why a ship could be detained in port. Surprisingly, Captain Forbes does not appear to have been severely censured, but the ultimate responsibility must rest with him. A captain at sea is entirely accountable for the safety of his ship and the welfare of his crew, and Forbes clearly failed on both counts on the return journey. Firstly, he should have taken on additional experienced seamen at Santa Rosalia. Secondly, when the loss of the lime-juice and foodstuffs came to light he should have sailed for the Falkland Islands or a South American port to replenish supplies and rest the crew. Thirdly, he should have acted swiftly to move his battered ship from the unsafe anchorage at Brandon. Finally, as soon as he arrived there he should have sought immediate medical attention for his sick, exhausted and starving crew.

The decision of the Court of Enquiry was a clear moral victory for the bereaved families, but justice would not be seen to be done until the owners paid them acceptable compensation. The latter at first repudiated liability but finally offered £50, which was increased to £75 when further pressure was applied. The families' advisers recommended prosecuting the owners, but William Baines and the other fathers had no stomach for the fight and the higher figure was accepted by most of the claimants. When it is considered that each apprentice had to pay a fee of £30 for his 'training' on the *Port Yarrock*, this was a miserable settlement. The widows and next of kin of the sailors fared no better.

The wreckage of the ship was auctioned shortly after the sinking, and over the next nineteen years much of the copper ore was salvaged. Also, as a direct result of the tragedy, Brandon Bay received a lifeboat service, a telegraph station and a coastguard station, the latter burned down by anti-Treaty forces in 1920. In 1994 there was a centenary commemoration organised by the local community and attended by some descendants of those who died. A variety of events took place, including the hanging of a wreath on the still-visible bowsprit of the ship.

7

The Achill boating tragedy of 1894

Achill, off the north-west coast of County Mayo, is the largest Irish island, with an area of 144 square kilometres. At the end of the nineteenth century it was a remote and poverty-stricken region, and the building of a bridge to the mainland in 1886 did little to improve matters. At that time the population was close on 5,000, but with only a small proportion of the land suitable for cultivation most people struggled to survive. In 1910 Paul Henry, who immortalised the landscape and its inhabitants in his paintings, described the harsh life as entirely traditional, the women working in the fields and bogs in addition to doing all the work of the house. He saw them as having no time for anything else and was constantly astonished by their cheerful acceptance of such a hard life because they were old before their time.

The pressure on the population was relieved somewhat each summer with the annual migration of mainly young men and girls to work on farms in Scotland and England. Such seasonal work provided an opportunity to settle outstanding debts and save some money for the winter. The work was mainly potato-harvesting and the only requirements were a strong back and a willingness to work. Hundreds of 'tatie-hokers', as they were known, left the island every year, and if all went well their earnings would make life easier for them and their families over the next twelve months. They travelled to Britain by steamship, but as there was no port in Achill where such a large vessel could dock they had to embark at Westport. Some of the younger people would walk the whole way, a distance of over 40 miles from the western part of the island. A visitor, writing in 1880, recalls meeting a group of twelve strong, cheerful, hearty-looking girls making such a journey in their bare feet, thus saving their boots, which they carried in their hands, for the harsh work ahead.

On Thursday 14 June 1894 the steamer *Elm* was anchored in calm water opposite Annagh Point, about a mile from Westpoint Pier. It was awaiting the arrival of four hookers, which had left Darby's Point in Achill Sound that morning, bringing hundreds of tatie-hokers for embarkation to Glasgow and the Scottish potato fields.

Nineteenth-century painting of hookers off the west coast, by Richard Brydges Beechey (courtesy of the Gorry Gallery, Dublin).

The Newport to Achill passenger train skirts Bellacragher Bay on its approach to Mulranny station *c.* 1906 (courtesy of the National Library of Ireland).

Those who had walked were already on board. The hooker is the centuries-old one-masted fishing-boat with large mainsail still popular on the west coast of Ireland and used for a variety of purposes, including the carriage of passengers. This was how the islanders were traditionally transported to Westport, with people packed into the hold of each vessel.

It was a fine, sunny day with a fair westerly wind when they left the island, and after an uneventful passage across Clew Bay the first of the hookers passed the *Elm* on course for Westport harbour. The next to arrive was the *Victory*, popularly known as 'Jack Healy's hooker', and as many of the young people on board had never seen a steamer before, they rushed up on deck laughing and shouting and exchanging jokes with the crew. Two or three minutes later this happy scene turned to tragedy, as the *Victory* was suddenly seen to heel over and capsize on its port side, whilst the mainsail settled down on the hold, trapping those below; the remainder were thrown into the water. Captain Carswell of the *Elm* immediately launched the steamer's four boats, to be joined later by the other hookers when they had landed their passengers, as well as some local craft. Despite their best efforts 32 people drowned, 25 of them female and one only twelve years of age. Many more would have died if the *Elm* had not been in the vicinity.

The majority of those who perished were landed at Westport the same day amidst scenes of lamentation, keening and moaning, but it was to be another two days before the *Victory* was refloated and the remaining victims brought ashore. Soon afterwards all the bodies, accompanied by 80 mourners, were taken to Newport by a train provided by the Midland Great Western railway. At that time there was no train service from Newport to Achill, but a line had recently been built, though not yet passed for traffic. It was decided, nevertheless, that an exception should be made to convey the coffins to the island. Thousands lined the route, and large numbers of men from the Royal Irish Constabulary were necessary to keep them off the line. The fifteen-mile journey took more than two hours and the train finally stopped some distance from Achill station, which was still under construction. Distressing scenes were witnessed as men, women and children crowded around the wagons to claim their lost relatives, and amid wild, unrestrained lamentations the bodies were taken to their homesteads to be waked. All were eventually buried in Kildowney old cemetery.

In the aftermath of the calamity the islanders were reminded of a grim prophecy made in the seventeenth century by a local man, Brian Rua O'Cearbhain, who had predicted that 'one day carriages on iron wheels emitting smoke and fire would come to Achill and their arrival and departure would be marked by death'. Two weeks before the line closed in 1937 this prediction was again regrettably fulfilled, when the bodies of ten boys from the Achill area who had been accidentally burnt to death in a locked dormitory on a potato farm near Glasgow were brought to the island by train from Dublin for burial.

Two days after the tragedy an inquest was held in Westport, but John (Jack) Healy, who had been at the helm of the *Victory* and survived, was so badly affected that he could not attend. He was criticised on three counts: first, that his boat was not properly ballasted; second, that it carried too many passengers; third, that when he changed course after passing the *Elm* he should have lowered, or at least reduced, sail. The court eventually decided, however, that the real cause of the capsizing was the sudden rush of people from the hold to the port side to see the steamer at the same time as it became necessary to alter course. Healy and the Sweeny family of Achill Sound, who jointly owned the hooker, were, perhaps fortunately, exonerated.

There was great sympathy throughout Ireland for the families of those who died, and a relief fund was immediately set up and generously supported. These events drew widespread attention to the poverty and deprivation in Achill, and the *Irish Weekly Independent* of 23 June 1894 wrote that

Memorial on the quay at Westport to the victims of the Achill boating tragedy.

'the poor people who were migrating to Scotland to gather in Scotch harvests were driven to quit their own homes by what a benevolent Liberal Chief Secretary lovingly termed the pinch of hunger. They had to go to Scotland to earn the landlord's rent and the seed rate, and all the other rates that an ameliorative British government imposed upon the very poor Irish for the benefit of British officials and the welfare of the British Empire. Otherwise, they would be evicted by due process of law which to the Irish peasant is another name for his own undoing.'

Regrettably, the early years of Irish independence did little to improve the islanders' lot, as the later tragedy of 1937 makes clear.

SAVING THE CREW OF THE *LEON XIII*

In April 1907 the square-sailed, steel-hulled, three-masted French vessel *Leon XIII* left Portland, Oregon, for Queenstown with a cargo of wheat. She was amongst the last of the wind-jammers to sail around Cape Horn, where bad weather and contrary winds delayed her passage, and she did not reach the Irish coast until the end of September, after a voyage of 158 days. Nearing Kinsale she was met by the local pilot boat with instructions to discharge her cargo in Limerick. The master, Captain Emile Lucas, steered his vessel around the Kerry coast and arrived at the mouth of the River Shannon about midday on Monday 30 September. Loop Head lighthouse was in sight when a great storm arose, blowing the ship off course. The north-westerly winds now became more violent, and the vessel, under three lower topsails, tried to tack off the coast but was driven towards the shore. The storm raged with fury throughout the night of Tuesday 1 October and all hands prepared for the worst. The following morning they saw land, and the captain decided to beach the ship as their only hope of safety. He headed for what seemed a safe strand, but about 600 metres from the shore opposite the small village of Quilty in County Clare they struck a reef, which broke the rudder and split the ship in two, although she remained wedged and afloat between two jagged rocks. All on board were safe, but Captain Lucas had broken a leg.

Early on the morning of 2 October a young fisherman, Michael McInerney, was the first to see the wreck and alerted the villagers, who rushed to the shore. They immediately launched their flimsy currachs in the hope of rescuing those on board, but the storm was so violent and the waves so high that they could make no progress towards the ship. All that day, powerless to help, they watched the unfortunate French sailors, who had neither food nor fresh water, cling to the wreckage as it was pounded by the waves. Darkness fell, and the crew with their injured captain endured a terrible night of sleet and rain, with the ever-present fear of being swept overboard. On shore the locals lit bonfires to show them that they had not been forgotten, and a candle burned in the window of every cottage.

HMS *Arrogant* comes to the rescue (courtesy of the National Library of Ireland).

Bell of the *Leon XIII* in Star of the Sea Church, Quilty.

The storm persisted all night and into the morning of 3 October. Fearful that the ship might soon break up, the fishermen of Quilty launched another rescue attempt, but the huge waves and surging seas foiled them again. Several currachs overturned, but all the men returned safely to shore amidst screams and lamentations from their womenfolk. Towards midday the storm abated but the seas continued to run high. Encouraged by the efforts to save them, the crew on the ship built a few makeshift rafts and when the currachs again braved the elements these were launched through a small gap in the reef. Some of the sailors clung to them and others swam behind, and as they approached the Quilty men they were snatched from the sea into the currachs. In this manner thirteen of the crew were brought safely to shore.

When night fell, Captain Lucas, his mate Louis Boutin, the cook and six sailors faced another terrible night on board. They found shelter in the forecastle, which was still above water, wrapped themselves in sails and ate their only source of sustenance—the wet salted wheat. From the outset the crew vowed not to desert their injured captain, for whom they obviously had great affection.

Salvation finally came in the early hours of 4 October, when the cruiser HMS *Arrogant*, dispatched by the admiral of the Atlantic fleet, steamed into the bay. It quickly launched its boats and the survivors were brought on board and landed in Queenstown the following day. The crew of the *Arrogant* raised a substantial sum of money, which they gave to the Frenchmen to help them on their journey home. They were also presented with boots and Royal Navy uniforms by the captain.

Meanwhile, back at Quilty the rescued seamen, two of whom were American and one English, were welcomed with open arms and given every attention by the villagers and people from the surrounding countryside. All were exhausted, cold, hungry and barely able to walk when dragged ashore, but so well were they cared for that two days later they seemed none the worse for their experience and were brought by motor car

Stained glass memorial at Star of the Sea
Church, Quilty.

Detail from a mural at Quilty National
School depicting the rescue.

to Spanish Point, where they were met by the French consular agent from Limerick, who fitted them out with new clothes and boots and gave them lunch in the Atlantic Hotel. There, one of the Americans, a striking young man with black ringlets falling around his shoulders, expressed great gratitude to their rescuers: 'We owe them our lives. I think God never made nobler creatures than your Quilty men. They are brave fellows all.' Later the mate was also fulsome in his praise: 'Ah!! Those Clare fishermen, they are heroic. They seemed to court death and risk their lives in the endeavour to save us.' That evening they left Spanish Point amid cheering crowds and later passed through Ennis on their way to Queenstown, where they were reunited with their comrades. All except Captain Lucas, who was still in hospital, returned to France on 11 October.

That is not the end of the story, however. The dramatic rescues received widespread press coverage, with particular emphasis on the bravery of the Quilty fishermen, and a fund was set up almost immediately to reward them. Contributions were received from many parts of Ireland but also from Canada, England, the United States and Australia. Amongst those who subscribed were Augustine Birral, chief secretary for Ireland,

William Redmond MP and the bishop of Killaloe, who gave the then very large sum of 50 pounds. When the fund was distributed to the 34 fishermen involved, a second was opened with the intention of building a church, as there was none in the poor village of Quilty at that time. This aim was soon achieved, and the present Star of the Sea Church was consecrated as the *Leon XIII* memorial chapel on Sunday 23 October 1910. The title was appropriate, as it bore the name not only of the wrecked ship but of a distinguished pope.

On 26 October 1908 the consular agent returned to Spanish Point and in front of an enthusiastic audience presented the fishermen, on behalf of the French government, with medals in recognition of their actions the year before. It was felt that there should also have been a monetary reward, and this omission was severely criticised in the French press.

A sister ship, *Le Marechal De Noailles*, launched the same day as the *Leon XIII*, also met her end in Ireland. On the night of 15 January 1913 she was stranded and wrecked close to the lighthouse at Mine Head, near Dungarvan, Co. Waterford.

REMEMBER THE *LUSITANIA*!

In the early years of the twentieth century the British Empire, the largest and most widely dispersed the world has ever known, was at the height of its power and prestige. With the Boer War won and the Royal Navy continuing to rule the waves as it had done since 1807, there seemed every reason to believe that another hundred years of imperial glory lay ahead. There were, however, storm clouds on the horizon.

Germany had many ties with England in war and in peace, and both royal families were closely related. Strains, however, appeared with the creation of a German empire by Bismarck in 1871, followed by rapid industrialisation, an aggressive armaments programme and the acquisition of colonies in Africa and elsewhere. There followed the creation of a powerful navy to rival the British, and this led to an arms race between the two countries and a profusion of new and powerful battleships. It also encouraged the development of the submarine, which previously had not been considered a serious war weapon. When hostilities finally broke out in August 1914, Great Britain had 75 ready for service, with a further 28 under construction. Germany had only 28 in service and 25 under construction, but these diesel-propelled vessels had the best range and depth performance in the world and each was capable of travelling some 5,000 miles. The U-boat (*Unterseeboot*) was to prove Germany's most powerful weapon in the coming naval war.

Complementing the arms race was a fierce rivalry for the Blue Riband of the Atlantic, first awarded in 1838 for the fastest crossing of that ocean. Until 1897 the honours had been shared by Great Britain and the United States, but in 1897 the German liner *Kaiser Wilhelm Der Grosse* broke the record, which was held by German liners for the next ten years. British pride was affronted, and it was in response to this perceived national humiliation that the *Lusitania* and her sister ship *Mauretania* were built. They were named after Roman Portugal and Roman Morocco and Algeria respectively.

With financial assistance from the British government, the Cunard Line ordered

British army recruiting poster.

their construction by the John Brown shipyard on the River Clyde, and the *Lusitania* was launched in 1907. She fulfilled all expectations and on her second Atlantic run brought the Blue Riband home. She captured the public's imagination from the outset and, along with the *Mauretania*, was the largest, fastest, most technologically advanced and sumptuous liner afloat. She received a tumultuous reception when she arrived in New York on her maiden voyage, and the newspapers raved about her speed, strength and safety. Huge crowds came to view the 30,396-ton, four-funnel, 785ft-long vessel with a crew of 850 and a passenger capacity of 2,000. She was lavishly fitted out and the third-class accommodation was superior to any ship afloat. One journalist described her as 'more beautiful than Solomon's temple and big enough to hold all his wives'.

For the next seven years she and the *Mauretania* were the queens of the North Atlantic, and the social prestige of sailing on either was tremendous. The *Titanic* would have stolen their thunder but for its untimely demise; no other liner could compare. With the advent of war in August 1914 the *Mauretania* was given a new role as a troop-transporter and hospital ship, but the *Lusitania* continued on the transatlantic run. She was under instruction, however, from the British Admiralty as to the course she was to follow, and her cargo space was at their disposal.

In February 1915 Germany announced a campaign of unrestricted submarine warfare, which put all enemy vessels, armed or unarmed, in danger. The ultimatum, considered barbaric by Britain and her allies, immediately put the *Lusitania* at risk, but the Admiralty believed that the Germans would not risk sinking any vessel on which citizens of the United States, then a neutral power, were passengers, as their death might force that country into declaring war. This complacent attitude was proved false on 1 May 1915, the very day the *Lusitania* was due to leave New York on what was to be her final voyage, when the following notice was placed in the *New York Times* by the Imperial German Embassy:

'Travellers intending to embark on the Atlantic voyage are reminded that a state of war exists between Germany and her allies and Great Britain and her allies; that the zone of war includes the waters adjacent to the British Isles; that, in accordance with formal notice given by the imperial German government, vessels flying the flag of Great Britain, or any of her allies, are liable to destruction in those waters *and that travellers sailing in this war zone on ships of Great Britain or her allies do so at their own risk.'*

The reaction of the 1,257 passengers was mixed. Some were fearful, while others

German U-boats at Kiel in 1914. In the foreground is U-20.

dismissed the warning as German propaganda. Most were reassured when told by Captain William Turner and his officers that the *Lusitania* could outrun any German vessel of war and, in any event, that the British Admiralty would take 'mighty good care of her'. Nevertheless, when the great ship finally moved into the Hudson River to commence her 102nd transatlantic crossing she left behind a small number of passengers who had decided not to travel or who switched to a neutral vessel.

The first full day at sea was a warm Sunday with bright sunshine, a calm sea and occasional sightings of porpoises. Passengers played deck games and indulged in a variety of other activities; Captain Turner conducted the usual Sunday religious service. If there was an underlying unease, the pleasant routine of a liner at sea made the war and its dangers appear remote to most of those on board. The food was excellent, especially in the magnificent double-tiered first-class dining-room, where only the finest dishes were served; there were parties, dancing and entertainment to suit most tastes every evening. With 129 children on board it must have been a lively ship.

The next four days passed in similar fashion and the good weather continued, but there was a growing sense of insecurity as they neared Ireland and the war zone. Passengers speculated about the possibility of the ship being attacked and wondered when they would see the promised Royal Navy escort. On the evening of Thursday 6 May Captain Turner had the first intimation of impending danger when he received a wireless message warning that submarines were active off the south coast of Ireland. That night, at a talent concert in aid of seamen's charities, he announced this news but assured his listeners that they would be securely in the care of the Royal Navy the following day and there was no need for alarm.

One of the submarines was U-20, commanded by 30-year-old Kapitan-Leutnant Walther Schwieger, an experienced seaman and an expert on submarine matters. His crew was four officers and 31 men. U-20 was a diesel-powered vessel, 210ft long with a 3.5in. gun and seven torpedoes, and had left its base in Germany for offensive action in the Irish Sea and its approaches the day before the *Lusitania* sailed. At the same time as Captain Turner was warning his passengers of possible danger, Kapitan Schwieger brought U-20 to the surface to recharge her batteries following a most successful day, during which he had sunk the British steamers *Centurion* and *Candidate*, both of 6,000 tons, off the coast of Waterford. He still had three torpedoes but was under orders to save at least two for the journey home, which meant that he had to be very sure of his next target.

Early the following morning, Friday 7 May, the *Lusitania* was forced to reduce speed because of dense fog and Captain Turner was so worried about his precise

Lusitania memorial at Cobh, Co. Cork.

position that he ordered depth soundings. He also ordered the fog-horn to be sounded every minute, which upset some of the passengers, as it betrayed the ship's position. Many were already highly nervous, and some had left their cabins the night before to sleep in the public rooms. About 10am, however, the fog lifted to reveal a beautiful day with light winds, a smooth sea and bright sunshine, which helped to dispel some of the gloom. All morning lookouts scanned the ocean for any sign of danger and the hoped-for Royal Navy escort but saw nothing. At 11am Turner received a wireless message from Valentia in County Kerry reading 'Submarines active in southern part Irish Channel; last heard of twenty miles south of Coninbeg Lightship'; this told him little more than he already knew but, amazingly, did not mention that the *Centurion* and the *Candidate* had been sunk near there the day before. In view of this information, however, he decided to move towards the land and altered his course accordingly. At 1.40pm the familiar outline of the Old Head of Kinsale appeared over the horizon and Turner was now aware of his exact position. He then altered course again and surviving passengers remembered that the change happened 'very quickly'. Two miles dead ahead and fast approaching was the U-20.

Kapitan Schwieger also encountered thick fog early on the same morning, which hampered his efforts to seek a final prize before returning to Germany. As the weather improved about 10am he spotted the out-of-date cruiser *Juno* making for Queenstown (Cobh), but although he gave chase he could not catch her. At 1.20pm, in beautiful weather, he saw coming over the horizon what he later described in his war diary as 'a large passenger liner with four funnels'. The submarine dived and began a steady approach at nine knots, during which their quarry changed course twice. When they were within two miles she was dead ahead and, at this stage, the experienced captain must have realised that his victim was the *Lusitania*. He never once hesitated, however, and when they were within 700 metres he launched a gyro-torpedo, which unleashed a trail of bubbles as it left the bow tube. It struck the liner below the bridge with great force, causing a huge explosion, closely followed by another further forward. Almost immediately the *Lusitania* listed to starboard as its bow dipped into the sea.

Just prior to the attack, most passengers were at lunch or relaxing in their cabins or in the lounge; others were on deck enjoying the lovely weather. All were looking forward to arriving in Liverpool the following day. Suddenly all hell broke loose, as almost 2,000 people found themselves in mortal danger and looked for a means of escape. The initial explosion had already killed some passengers and crew, while others were badly injured by flying debris and escaping steam; a few were trapped in the lifts, from which there was no means of escape. Many became hysterical and panic-stricken; others were so shocked that they were incapable of action. Most, however, stayed calm and put on the lifebelts and preservers supplied by the crew, who, with some exceptions, did all they could to save life. There was particular concern for the children.

On the bridge, Captain Turner tried desperately to slow his floundering vessel and steer for the land, but without success. Realising that she was doomed, he gave orders to abandon ship and lower the lifeboats, women and children first. Only one was launched on the port side owing to the list. On the starboard side it was less difficult, but some boats capsized or were damaged as they hit the water. A few were upended on the way down, spilling their occupants into the sea. Smashed boats dangled vertically from their davits. A small number of collapsible boats were launched but proved of limited value.

As the ship's list worsened, people dived off the rails or jumped into the sea 60ft below. Others tried to slide down ropes or wire, including the log line. Suddenly the lurching and rolling ship plunged abruptly, and foaming water came rushing in over the forecastle. At this stage the crew were also fleeing for their lives, with Captain Turner a lonely figure climbing the ladder to the top bridge. Many people were still trapped on board as the stern reared higher into the air and the propellers and rudder became visible. The *Lusitania*—queen of the Atlantic Ocean and greyhound of the seas—then went into a slow dive by the head and hit the seabed some 340ft below, twelve miles from the Old Head of Kinsale. To one survivor it sounded like 'the

The *Lusitania c.* 1910.

collapse of a great building during a fire'. A mere eighteen minutes had elapsed since the torpedo struck.

The majority of those still on board perished during the final dive, during which there was a violent underwater explosion. A mound of foaming water sent swimmers, corpses and wreckage of every kind to the surface. As the sea calmed on a still-beautiful day, the debris of cargo, broken furniture and the like interspersed with dead bodies spread for miles in the sea. Probably as many as 1,500 still struggled to remain alive. Class no longer mattered, as stockbrokers, society ladies, stokers and bellboys found themselves in the same lifeboats or sharing a piece of wreckage in an effort to remain afloat. All now hoped that help would soon arrive. An SOS message had been sent soon after the attack and was received by stations all along the coast.

The first boat to come to the rescue was the *Wanderer* (also known as *Peel 12*), a small Isle of Man trawler fishing for mackerel three miles away. On arrival, she rescued 220 people from four lifeboats and then, laden to capacity, took two more lifeboats in tow. Two Irish fishing-boats arrived at the scene an hour or so later. The *Daniel O'Connell* picked up 65 survivors, mainly women and children, while the *Elizabeth* rescued a similar number, many in a very weak condition. All three vessels made for Kinsale, the nearest port, but at the mouth of the harbour they were stopped by the captains of government tugs, who demanded that those they had rescued be transferred to their vessels for passage to Queenstown, at least an hour and a half away. All three captains protested, as they were only twenty minutes from Kinsale, but for some inexplicable reason they were overruled and the transfer took place.

The relief vessels from Queenstown only began to arrive about 6pm, three and a half hours after the SOS was received. The rescue itself was described by one observer as 'late, inadequate and chaotic'. By this time hundreds of those unable to gain the relative safety of the lifeboat had died from drowning, injuries or the cold sea. Many still alive were in a deplorable condition and would not survive much longer. The Courtmacsherry lifeboat with twelve crew on board rowed for three and a half hours to reach the disaster area, by which time few people in the water were still alive. They were shocked to see the number of corpses floating on the sea, many horribly mutilated. Some mothers still clasped their babies in a deathly embrace.

When the first of the rescue vessels arrived in Queenstown, the townspeople were horrified at the traumatised state of the survivors. One eyewitness saw 'bruised and shuddering women, crippled and half-clothed men and a few wide-eyed little children'. Another was distressed at the sight of 'helpless, half-clad, soaked and shivering women, with husbands looking for their wives and fathers for their children'. A seaman who had been in the water for five and a half hours staggered

Sir Hugh Lane by John Singer Sargent (courtesy of Dublin City Gallery: The Hugh Lane).

ashore in a terrible condition, his eyes so closed with mucus that he believed he had gone blind. Many, alive when they came ashore, died later of exposure or of their terrible injuries. One of those to reach shore alive was Captain Turner, who, washed off the bridge as the *Lusitania* sank, swam towards some wreckage, where he remained for several hours with a crewman who helped to support him until a rescue boat arrived. An observer heard him remark as he came ashore, 'It is the fortune of war'.

Rescue boats continued to arrive throughout the night but increasing numbers carried as many corpses as survivors, while the last to dock had only dead bodies on board. The final death toll was 1,198, of whom 128 were Americans, including the multi-millionaire Alfred Vanderbilt, who had behaved gallantly whilst helping women and children to the lifeboats. The Irishman Sir Hugh Lane, art expert and director of the National Gallery of Ireland, also died. Neither body was ever recovered. As the number of dead reaching Queenstown increased, temporary morgues were set up in the town hall and elsewhere.

The local inhabitants did all in their power to help the traumatised and exhausted survivors. Hotels and private houses opened their doors and provided food, clothes and blankets. Doctors and nurses worked all night to relieve the suffering. They could do little, however, for those who had lost their nearest and dearest and struggled to come to terms with the terrible scenes they had witnessed. This was a type of disaster of which few, if any, of those involved had prior experience. Nothing quite like it had been seen in Ireland before.

Over the next few days the burial of the dead became a matter of urgency, and horse-drawn hearses, carts and coffins poured into Queenstown from every part of County Cork. Soldiers dug three huge graves in the old church cemetery two miles north of the town, and on Monday 10 May the funeral procession of over 140 unidentified victims wound its way past thousands of silent local people to their final resting place. A military band played Chopin's *Funeral March* and the route was lined with soldiers from three Irish regiments. At the graveyard, services were conducted by Catholic and Protestant clergymen, while muffled drums rolled and the hymn *Abide with me* was sung. Sailors then lowered the coffins into the graves.

Where it was possible to identify the bodies of the deceased, they were embalmed for later collection by relatives. At the same time the search continued all along the coast for the many people still missing, but only a small number of bodies were recovered and the sea eventually claimed over 900 of those who died.

The *Lusitania* had been sunk in circumstances contrary to the rules of war at the time, and the deaths of so many innocent men, women and children caused an outburst of anti-German feeling in many parts of the

Tombstone in the Old Church Cemetery, Cobh, commemorating a *Lusitania* victim.

world, particularly in the United States. When Captain Schwieger arrived home he was given a hero's welcome, but it was not long before the Germans realised that the sinking was a colossal blunder. Much of the blame was attributed to the Kaiser personally—so much so that he ordered a ban on attacking passenger liners in future. Numerous heated diplomatic exchanges took place between the American and German governments, with many people in the United States of the opinion that honour required a declaration of war. In fact, despite the loss of many more American lives owing to U-boat sinkings, the United States did not enter the war until 31 July 1917. It is significant, however, that many of their soldiers went into action to shouts

Captain William Turner.

of 'Remember the *Lusitania*!'. The death of their compatriots on that tragic day was the catalyst that led them to war.

Over the years there has been much controversy about whether the German attack was justified. The latter claimed that the liner was armed and carried Canadian troops, but neither accusation was true. They also said that it carried munitions, which the British denied, but we now know that the cargo included 1,250 cases of shrapnel shells, over 4,000,000 Remington rifle cartridges and 46 tons of fine ammunition powder used in the manufacture of nitrate-based explosives. The real problem was the death of so many innocent civilians at a time when they were not directly targeted in war, as is the case today. In this light it could be said that the sinking of the *Lusitania* marked the beginning of a new type of warfare, in which no distinction is made between the military and civilians, and both are equally at risk. Coventry, Dresden and Hiroshima come readily to mind, as does the attack on the Twin Towers in New York in the present century.

Captain Schwieger died in September 1917 when his submarine, the larger and more powerful U-88, was destroyed by British mines in the North Sea and all on board were killed. He was a brilliant and ruthless commander, well liked by those who served under him, and waged unrestricted war in accordance with the instructions of his superior officers. So single-minded was he in this respect that he even ignored the Kaiser's order not to sink any more passenger ships when he torpedoed the liner *Hesperian* in September 1915 and the liner *Cymric* the following year. Shortly before his death he was awarded the Pour Le Mérite medal, the highest honour a German naval officer could receive, for his unflinching sense of duty and in recognition of the 190,000 tons of allied shipping he had sunk. There is, nevertheless, evidence that he may have suffered pangs of conscience and a sense of guilt for sinking the *Lusitania*. When the war was over, his fiancée described a visit from him shortly after that happened when he was 'so haggard, so silent and so different' that she knew immediately that something was wrong. In this connection it is perhaps significant that Schwieger did not allow his comrades to look through the periscope in the aftermath of the attack, possibly because the sight was too horrifying. War often makes impossible demands on young men like Schwieger. In the end he became a victim himself.

Kapitan-Leutnant Walther Schwieger.

There was much criticism of the Royal Navy for their failure to provide any kind of protection, and the Admiralty diverted attention by laying most of the blame on Captain Turner, despite his previous outstanding record. At the official enquiry a month after the sinking he was accused of disobeying orders, ignoring warnings and behaving in a negligent and reckless manner. The First Sea Lord, Admiral Jackie Fisher, even went so far as to suggest that he might have been in the pay of the Germans. Turner, who might have been suffering from post-traumatic shock, seemed confused by some of the questions, but in the end the verdict of Lord Mersey, who chaired the enquiry, was that the whole blame lay with the Germans. The reality was that the *Lusitania* became a victim of complacency and neglect on the part of the Admiralty, whose only excuse could have been that at the time they were heavily involved in the Dardanelles and elsewhere. Turner resumed his naval career in command of the liner *Ivernia* and again survived when it was sunk in 1917 off Cape Matapan in Greece. This earned him the distinction of having two great liners sunk under him and living to tell the tale. After the war he was promoted to commodore of the Cunard Line and awarded the OBE, but he never forgot his scapegoating at the hands of the Admiralty and is said to have died a bitter man, aged 76, in 1933. His grave overlooks the Mersey Estuary.

The *Lusitania* was torpedoed on 7 May 1915. Exactly 30 years later, on 7 May 1945, the American General Dwight Eisenhower accepted the surrender of the German armies in the West and the war in Europe ended. The slate had finally been wiped clean.

10

THE SAD FATE OF THE *LEINSTER*

The Royal Mail steamer *Leinster* was one of four identical twin-screw steamers launched in 1896 and 1897 by the City of Dublin Steam Packet Company. The others were named *Ulster*, *Munster* and *Connaught*, and they were the four fastest channel steamers in the world at that time. They were the main means of travel between Ireland and Great Britain and operated from Kingstown to Holyhead in north Wales. In addition to passengers, each carried up to 30 postal workers and 250 bags of mail; during the two-and-a-half-hour journey the mail was sorted and was ready for delivery by the time they reached port.

During the first three years of the Great War the service continued more or less as usual, but in 1917 the *Connaught* was requisitioned as a troop ship and was subsequently torpedoed and sunk in the English Channel. In the same year the *Ulster* and the *Munster* were occasionally used for the same purpose. An increasing number of military personnel were also travelling by the ordinary mail service, which thus became a potential target for German submarines entering the Irish Sea. Such activity increased in 1918, and all three remaining steamers were attacked but not hit that year. As a result, escort vessels were necessary but in practice only operated at the discretion of the Admiralty. These were usually British and American destroyers supported by seaplanes and airships.

The steamers' luck held until 10 October 1918. That morning the submarine U-123, commanded by Oberleutnant Robert Ramm, lay submerged close to the Kish light-vessel, some twelve miles east of Kingstown. At about 8.30am the *Ulster* was sighted on her way home from Holyhead and he made ready to attack. It veered away, however, as part of the zigzag course the ships adopted to avoid submarines, and the opportunity was lost. An hour or so later the *Leinster* came into view, *en route* from Kingstown on a course that would take it straight across his bow. There were 771 people on board, including 489 soldiers, 180 civilians and 22 postal workers. Despite the strong military presence, including high-ranking officers, she had no escort and

A postcard of the *Leinster*.

when sighted would appear not to have commenced the recommended zigzagging routine.

Ramm's first torpedo passed harmlessly across the bow of the *Leinster* but was seen from the bridge. A second soon followed, and although the ship tried to take evasive action it was struck on the port side in the vicinity of the mailroom, the torpedo passing through to the starboard side, where it caused further damage. The commander, Captain William Birch, immediately gave orders to abandon ship and the crew began to lower the lifeboats. A short time later a second torpedo struck on the starboard side and a full lifeboat being lowered at the time was blown to pieces. Another, already launched, was overturned by the explosion and most of the hundred or so on board died. A total of two or three lifeboats and about twelve life-rafts were successfully launched by the time the *Leinster* began to sink bow first with her stern high in the air. According to one survivor, she went down with 'a hissing sound' and suddenly disappeared. Barely 90 minutes had elapsed since she left Kingstown.

Probably half of those who set sail that morning were now dead following the explosion that ripped the ship apart. The lucky ones were in the lifeboats or on the rafts, but the majority of those still alive struggled to remain afloat in a rough sea in what was described as 'dirty weather'. Some managed to board the rafts; others clung to the wreckage from the ship. Many clung to the sides of the lifeboats and rafts while still in the water. The terrible scenes can only be imagined as one by one those in the water drowned or lost consciousness, often in the presence of their nearest and dearest. Eventually only those who had found some way of supporting themselves were left alive. They hoped that they would survive the intense cold and shock until someone came to their rescue. Many were injured, including Captain Birch, whose legs were broken when he was thrown from the bridge into the sea when the second torpedo struck.

Fortunately, an SOS message had been sent when the first torpedo struck. At the time there were three destroyers on patrol off the coast, and as soon as they received the signal they altered course in a 6–7 force wind. The first to arrive at the scene was HMS *Malland*, which lost its fore bridge on the way owing to heavy seas. It lowered its whaler and with great difficulty rescued nineteen men and two women. HMS *Lively* attempted to rescue those in one of the lifeboats, but in the process the latter capsized and many of its occupants, including Captain Birch, died. Others were eventually taken on board, along with people on or clinging to rafts. In all, they saved 102 men, 24 women and a child. HMS *Seal* also launched its whaler and a skiff, but the latter was swamped and sunk by the scores of people who tried to climb on board. The whaler picked up as many people as it could hold but as they were being

One of the *Leinster's* two anchors, part of the public memorial on the sea front at Dun Laoghaire.

hoisted into the destroyer it was stove in against the ship's side and swamped. Hundreds of people were still in the water and many were crushed to death as the warship began to roll violently in the heavy sea. Lifelines were flung into the water and some were saved in this way, but in the end only 47 men, five women and a child were rescued. Other vessels, including the armed patrol yacht *Helga* (famous for its role in the 1916 Rising), also saved lives, and a total of 270 people survived the sinking. Nevertheless, 501 had died, making this the greatest local marine disaster in Ireland's history. The majority who lost their lives were from Ireland or other parts of the British Isles, but a substantial number of the military were from Australia, New Zealand, Canada and the United States. One of those who survived was a senior American naval officer, Captain Hutch Ingram Cone, but he sustained injuries that resulted in permanent physical disability. He retired from the navy in 1922 with the rank of rear admiral, and in 1945 the destroyer USS *Cone* was named in his honour.

There were many acts of individual bravery. An outstanding example is provided by William Maher, a 33-year-old veteran of the Boer War and a fireman on the

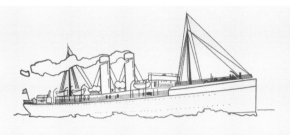

R.M.S. *LEINSTER*

This plaque is erected to the memory of the twenty one Dublin Post Office staff who died when the mail boat *Leinster* was torpedoed en route from Dun Laoghaire to Holyhead on the tenth of October 1918. The men were among the five hundred and one civilians, soldiers and sailors who lost their lives in one of Ireland's greatest maritime disasters.

Charles Archer	John Ledwidge
Jennings Attwooll	Albert MacDonnell
James Blake	William Maxwell
Tom Bolster	Patrick Murphy
Joseph Bradley	William Pasker
Mathew Brophy	Richard Patterson
Peter Daly	Joseph Robinson
John Dewar	Adam Smyth
John Dolan	William Wakefield
Patrick Forbes	James Warbrook
Michael Hogan	

Memorial in Dun Laoghaire post office to the 21 Dublin postal workers who lost their lives.

Leinster. When he was hurled into the sea, he helped Mrs Louisa Toppin and her thirteen-year-old daughter Dorothy onto a raft, and with his encouragement and cheerfulness helped them to survive for two and a half hours until help arrived. By that time five of the people with them had been washed away by the heavy seas, and their only other companion was a private soldier. When the launch reached them, Mrs Toppin lost consciousness, but Maher managed to get her on board together with the soldier. During this operation, however, the raft capsized and Dorothy was washed away. Despite his exhausted condition, Maher swam to her rescue and managed to haul her on board also. Mrs Toppin said later that without his assistance both she and her daughter would have perished, and in 1919 the Royal Humane Society in London awarded him a silver medal. Dorothy Toppin also gave him a watch with the inscription 'To William Maher from Dorothy Toppin. As a small token of gratitude for saving her life. Leinster disaster 10th October 1918'.

Second Lieutenant Hugh Love Parker also displayed great courage. Having been wounded in France early in 1918, he had only partial use of one arm and was appointed adjutant to the *Leinster* to deal with any problems involving servicemen on board. When the first torpedo struck he reported to Captain Birch, who told him to go to the chart room and bring him the weighted books. After that, Birch instructed

Mrs Maud Marsham Rae.

him to give orders for the rafts to be released. This duty completed, he returned to the bridge for further orders, but the Captain replied, 'No, Mr Parker, I have to thank you very much, you have done your duty, there is nothing more to do, it is now everyone for themselves'. Shortly afterwards the second torpedo struck, but Parker managed to lower himself from the upended rear of the ship onto the last of the lifeboats. It was so crowded, however, that he jumped overboard and swam to a nearby raft. As he moved towards it he realised that a woman, Mrs Maud Marsham Rae, was holding on to his leg, and he managed to get her on board and pulled himself up. Shortly afterwards Mrs Rae saw her husband clinging to an upturned boat; he shouted to Parker, 'For God's sake look after my wife!', after which they lost contact. Also on the raft were two sailors and four soldiers, but two of the latter succumbed to the severe cold and buffeting waves and were lost overboard. Parker supported the lady for one and three-quarter hours until they were eventually rescued with great difficulty by HMS *Mallard*. Her soldier husband did not survive. Having seen Mrs

The RMS *Leinster* in camouflage, by William Minshall Birchall (1884–1941) (courtesy of Michael Charles and the British Mercantile Marine Memorial Collection).

Rae safely ashore in Kingstown, the remarkable Lieutenant Parker walked to a hotel and in his subsequent report remarked that 'he personally felt no worse for his experience'. He too was awarded a silver medal by the Royal Humane Society.

It might be expected that a disaster on this scale occurring only a small distance from the capital city would have a huge impact on the population in general. But instead an apparent amnesia set in, and for over 70 years not a single public memorial was erected in memory of those who died. The principal reason was the nature of the Irish Free State that replaced the British in 1922. It wished to perpetuate the myth of unremitting Irish resistance to British rule over the centuries, and therefore the involvement of Irish men and women in the British Forces was written out of Irish history. The sinking of the *Leinster* became part of the collective memory loss. Other reasons were the tendency of historians to understate the number of those who died and the lack of information about them.

Towards the end of the twentieth century, however, and largely thanks to such journalists as Kevin Myers and Philip Lecane, there was a growing realisation that a major injustice had been done to those Irish men and women who had served in the two World Wars. At the same time the fog of amnesia surrounding the *Leinster* gradually lifted. In 1991 one of its anchors was recovered and placed near Carlisle Pier, Dun Laoghaire, where on 29 January 1996 it was dedicated as a memorial by the Minister of State for the Marine. In 2003 a plaque in memory of the 21 postal workers who had died was unveiled in Dun Laoghaire post office. On 10 October of the same year the Irish naval vessel LE *Aoife* approached the site of the wreck at the same time as four Royal Air Force jets from Anglesey in a joint commemoration.

It is fitting that we also remember the fate of submarine U–123 and its young crew. Its commander, Robert Ramm, was 27, his first officer 23 and his second officer 21, while the average age of their subordinates was about twenty. They were relatively inexperienced and were sent on their offensive mission at a time when the German navy was on the verge of mutiny and their superiors knew that the war was lost. It is unlikely, however, that Ramm and his men had any idea that hostilities were soon to cease. They were simply doing their duty, carrying out orders and hoping to survive. They never made it home, however, as ten days after they sank the *Leinster* they struck a mine off the Orkney Islands and all on board were killed. Neither sinking had the slightest effect on the outcome of the war.

11

DISASTER ON THE SHORT SEA ROUTE

Prior to 1872, the shortest passenger mail-boat service between Ireland and Britain was from Donaghadee in County Down to Portpatrick in south-west Scotland, a distance of only 22 miles. With the coming of the railway to Stranraer, however, and trains arriving there from London and Glasgow, the crossing was changed from that port to Larne in County Antrim, a distance of 36 miles known as the short sea route.

Between 1872 and 1953 four passenger ships named *Princess Victoria* made the crossing on a regular basis. The last so named went into service in 1947 and was the first car ferry with roll-on/roll-off facilities to operate between Ireland and Britain. There had been similar ships on other routes since the 1930s, but otherwise cars had to be hoisted on board by crane and only a few could be carried at the one time. In 1949 the car deck of the new ship was strengthened to allow the carriage of 12-ton milk tankers, and at the same time a spray door that could be raised and lowered was fitted to the stern. The transportation of milk from Northern Ireland to England, known as 'the milk run', was very profitable, and tankers took precedence over private cars. In October 1949, as she crossed from Larne with high seas running, some of the tankers broke loose, causing the ship to take on a 10° list, but she eventually reached Stranraer safely. In September 1950 the stern doors were dented as she berthed at the same port, but repairs put her quickly back into service. In November 1951 on passage from Stranraer she encountered heavy seas, and waves breached the stern doors and flooded the car deck, forcing the ship to anchor; it took one and a half hours to remove the water. None of these incidents led to any action by the owners, the British Transport Commission. Their failure in this respect was to have tragic consequences.

Early on the morning of Saturday 31 January 1953 Captain James Ferguson cycled from his home overlooking the pier at Stranraer and took command of the *Princess Victoria* for the journey to Larne. High winds had prevented the loading of any vehicles, but 44 tons of cargo was stored in the car deck. The weather forecast

A stem view of the *Princess Victoria*.

The *Princess Victoria* (courtesy of the National Library of Ireland).

spoke of a gale moderating to strong winds, and while Ferguson knew that the passage would be unpleasant he had no reason to expect exceptionally severe weather. On board were 127 passengers and 49 crew.

At 7.45am the *Princess Victoria* sailed up Lough Ryan. Then, with frightening speed, the weather worsened, snow began to fall and the ship had barely reached the open sea when trouble began. The wind was from the north-west and mountainous seas, 20–30ft high, began to batter her. Then came a wave, bigger than the others, which burst open the steel doors in the stern. Some of the crew managed to close them, but they remained shut for only a few minutes, after which a large volume of water poured into the car deck. The captain tried to manoeuvre back to the relative safety of Lough Ryan but could do little except use his engine to keep her head into the wind. In this way he held his position off Corsewall Point, a few miles from the entrance to the lough, but water continued to pour in and the *Princess Victoria* began to list to starboard. It was now 9.45am and a radio message was sent to Portpatrick:

The only lifeboat to remain afloat shelters in the lee of the tanker *Pass of the Drumochter.*

'Hove to off mouth of Lough Ryan. Vessel not under command. Car deck flooded. Heavy list to starboard. Urgent assistance of tugs required.' No tugs were able to put to sea, but the Portpatrick lifeboat *Jeanie Spiers* was launched at 11am and set a course northwards. At about the same time the destroyer HMS *Contest* left her moorings in Rothesay Bay and headed for the same area.

They arrived too late, as the wind and seas had already taken control of the *Princess Victoria*, which was now drifting on a south-westerly course towards the Irish coast. Despite the huge amount of water on her car deck and the increasing list to starboard, she managed to stay afloat for four hours from the time the first SOS was sent. Survivors reported that the passengers were very quiet and there was no panic, but many must have feared the worst. At 13.08 a message was sent indicating that her engine had stopped, and it must have been about this time that a fireproof door giving access to a corridor leading to the first-class lounge gave way and water spilled into that area and the adjoining cabin accommodation. This decided their fate, and at 13.54 the radio officer tapped out the message 'Estimated position now 5 miles east of Copeland's entrance Belfast Lough—on beam end'. Life-jackets had already been issued to passengers and crew and the lifeboats still above water had been prepared for launching. The fastenings of the life-rafts were also struck away. A final message from Captain Ferguson stated: 'One side of my ship is under water and the raging sea is the worst in my memory'. At 2pm the order was given to abandon ship, and ten minutes later the *Princess Victoria* sank. As she did so, three of her lifeboats lifted free from their davits and two of them drifted clear of the ship. The third, filled with male and female passengers and children, was almost free when the sea lifted and flung it, bow on, against the hull. This caused it to overturn, and those on board were hurled into the sea. All around were people held up by their white life-jackets, desperately trying to reach the rafts floating nearby.

Three hours had elapsed since the *Jeanie Spiers* and HMS *Consort* had set out on their rescue mission, and it was 1pm before they became aware that the stricken vessel was nearing the County Down coast; both set course for the Copeland Islands. The Donaghadee lifeboat *Sir Samuel Kelly* had also been launched, and four ships sheltering in Belfast Lough sailed to the rescue. One of them, the *Orchy*, a coastal cargo ship, sighted wreckage about five miles east of Mew Island, and the first of the survivors were found about fifteen minutes after the *Princess Victoria* sank. These were 29 men in one of the lifeboats, who were sheltered by the tanker *Pass of Drumochter* until the Donaghadee lifeboat arrived and took them on board. Six men in the other lifeboat were rescued by HMS *Consort*, which also saved a man from a raft; five others were rescued from rafts by the Portpatrick lifeboat. All the women on board the *Princess Victoria* died, as did Captain Ferguson, who stayed on the bridge as the ship sank, his officers and Major J. Maynard Sinclair, deputy prime minister of Northern Ireland. In spite of heroic efforts by the rescue ships, the gale-force winds, poor visibility and mountainous seas made their task almost impossible. The final death toll came to 133, making this the worst peacetime disaster on the Irish coast in the twentieth century.

The inquiry into the loss of the *Princess Victoria* opened in Belfast on 23 March 1953 and the court issued its judgement on 11 June the same year. This stated that the loss of the ship was due to her unseaworthy condition and laid the responsibility at the door of the British Transport Commission in that they:

- failed to provide stern doors sufficiently strong to withstand the onslaught of the heavy seas which may be reasonably expected to occur from time to time in the North Channel;
- failed to provide adequate freeing arrangements for seas which might enter the car space from any source; and
- failed to take precautionary steps after the incidents of October 1949 and November 1951.

The British Transport Commission appealed the findings of the court, but the appeal was dismissed on the grounds that they had not discharged their Common Law Duty

Captain James Ferguson at the wheel of the *Princess Victoria* (courtesy of the National Library of Ireland).

to take care and provide a seaworthy ship.

Warm tributes were paid to the crew and the manner in which they had behaved during their long ordeal. In their summing-up the court remarked that 'if the *Princess Victoria* had been as staunch as the men who manned her, then all would have been well and the disaster averted'. The radio officer David Broadfoot was posthumously awarded the George Cross in recognition of his selfless conduct in remaining at his post when he must have known that he was ruling out any chances of escape. Each of the coxswains of the Donaghadee and Portpatrick lifeboats received the British Empire Medal, and medals were also awarded to the captains of the other ships that came to the rescue.

When he sailed on that fateful Saturday morning, Captain Ferguson had no idea that the greatest storm to hit northern Europe in the twentieth century was on its way. It swept from the Atlantic Ocean, with winds reaching over 100 miles an hour at times, and coincided with a high spring tide. The almost enclosed North Sea could not get rid of the water being pressed in by tide and wind through its northern channels, and the coasts of eastern England and Holland took a terrible battering. The sea defences were no match for the storm, and much of the coastline of Norfolk, Suffolk, Essex and Kent was flooded, with enormous damage to property; over 300 people died, along with thousands of animals. In Holland the dykes were breached and more than a million people were forced to leave their homes; over 2,000 died. In retrospect it seems remarkable that anyone survived the sinking of the *Princess Victoria* in those terrible seas and Arctic-like conditions.

12

The cruel sea

Much of the great loss of life described in the previous chapters is remembered by public memorials, the majority erected in the past twenty years, yet this represents only a tiny number of those who have died in the seas around Ireland.

In the parish of Goleen near Mizen Head, Co. Cork, they can name over 40 vessels sunk on the short stretch of coast from Crookhaven to Three Castle Head, including the French frigate *L'Impatiente*, wrecked off the south side of Mizen Head in 1796 with the loss of 553 lives. Innumerable small craft were lost in the same area, including the pleasure-trawler *Taurima*, owned by former taoiseach Charles Haughey, which struck just below the lighthouse in 1985. All aboard were saved with the help of the light-keepers. Another sinking in the same vicinity occurred in 2007, when an inflatable boat used by a gang convicted of the biggest-ever drug shipment up to that time capsized in Dunlough Bay as they tried to bring their haul of cocaine ashore.

In the five-year period between 1877 and 1881, 52 vessels were wrecked on the County Down coast. Dundrum Bay, in particular, was a graveyard for ships over the centuries, and in October 1838 four vessels were lost there in a single day. The most memorable casualty in the bay was Isambard Brunel's *Great Britain*, which drove ashore in poor visibility on the night of 22 September 1846. This famous ship, the first large vessel to be driven by screw-propellers, was sailing from Liverpool to New York with 180 passengers when she went off course on her first day at sea, and in bad weather ran aground on Tyrella beach. Early efforts to free her failed, and a massive breakwater of faggots had to be built to protect her from winter gales. She was eventually refloated with great difficulty and huge expense the following summer. Today, in dry dock at Bristol, she is a major tourist attraction. Another famous ship, the Irish-owned *Sirius*, became the first vessel powered by steam to cross the Atlantic from Europe to America, beating Brunel's *Great Western* by a mere five hours. Sadly, she met an inglorious end when she was wrecked on the rocks at Ballycotton, Co. Cork, in January 1847.

The sinking of HMS *Vanguard* (courtesy of the National Library of Ireland).

The steam vessel *Sirius*.

Those who go to sea to fish for a living work in a dangerous environment. Prior to the Second World War, when the local waters teemed with fish and almost every harbour had a fishing fleet, drownings were commonplace and, not unlike road deaths today, often unreported. There were no reliable weather forecasts, safety precautions were rudimentary if they existed at all, vessels at sea had no contact with the land, rescue services were limited or arrived too late and few of those who went to sea could swim. Safety has greatly improved in the past 60 years but tragedies still occur, as off Hook Head, Co. Wexford, on 10 January 2007, when the fishing-boat *Père Charles* sank with the loss of five lives.

On 28 October 1927 a freak hurricane hit the coast of counties Galway and Mayo. During the early part of that day the weather had been good, and the local fishermen went to sea in the late afternoon in calm conditions. Suddenly and without warning the sky darkened and a ferocious storm lashed the coast. Terrified fishermen tried frantically to reach the safety of the shore, but the waves were so high and the wind so strong that it was impossible to row, and with loss of control many boats overturned and sank or crashed on cliffs or rocky shores. Others, more fortunate, drifted to a safe landfall. The storm abated the same evening and calm conditions

La Surveillante in a tableau at Bantry House, Co. Cork.

returned, but the loss of life was horrendous and the 'West Coast Disaster', as it is still known in the area, is thought to be the worst recorded single fishing disaster in Irish history. Seventeen died near Rossadelisk, Cleggan Bay, Co. Galway, and another ten at Inishbofin Island off the same county. A similar number were lost near Inishkea Island off County Mayo, and nine others in Lacken Bay on the north Mayo coast. In all, at least 49 fishermen died, and the desperately poor communities to which they belonged never fully recovered. The *Western People* described the day as 'Black Friday', and local tradition in Lacken tells of thousands of squealing seals arriving in the area the morning after the tragedy as if in sympathy.

Whiddy Island, Bantry Bay, Co. Cork, was the scene of two French naval disasters. On 15 December 1796 a fleet of 48 warships and transports sailed from Brest with 13,000 soldiers on board for an invasion of Ireland. Almost immediately they met heavy weather and many ships suffered storm damage. When they eventually reached their destination of Bantry Bay, the weather was so bad that it was impossible to land the troops and they were forced to return to France; had they been able to come ashore the history of Ireland and Great Britain may well have been different. One ship that never made it back home was the 32-gun state-of-the-art frigate *La*

Memorial to those from Lacken, Co. Mayo, who lost their lives in the great storm of 28 October 1927.

Surveillante, one of the earliest French vessels to have her hull copper-sheathed. This did not save her, however, and she was leaking so badly when she anchored off Whiddy Island that the crew and cavalry on board had to be transferred to other ships, after which she was scuttled. She was not seen again for another 183 years.

On 7 January 1979 a very different French vessel docked at Whiddy Island. This was the oil tanker *Betelgeuse* with 120,000 tons of fuel oil on board, two thirds of which were unloaded at the island terminal the same day. In the early hours of the following morning, unloading was continuing when a fire ignited in the ship's hull. Efforts were being made to bring it under control when there was an explosion on the tanker which split it in two, sending flames and debris to a height of 1,000ft. A huge rescue operation was launched, but the sea around the doomed vessel was ablaze while acrid black smoke belched from the hull, making it very difficult for the fire-fighting tugs. When the fire was eventually brought under control, it was found that the entire crew of 42 had died, along with eight local workers, making this the worst naval disaster on the coast of the Republic of Ireland since Independence in 1922. The quarter-mile jetty was rebuilt and over a period of about eighteen months the wreck of the *Betelgeuse* was removed. During the latter work divers discovered the

The SS *Great Britain* dropping her pilot (artist: Joseph Walter).

remains of the *La Surveillante*.

In the aftermath of the Napoleonic Wars many regiments in the British army returned to barracks in Ireland. In June 1816 the troop ships *Seahorse, Boadicea* and *Lord Melville* sailed from Ramsgate in Kent for Cork, with soldiers and their wives and children on board. While crossing the Irish Sea they encountered bad weather with violent easterly gales, and all three were driven ashore and wrecked. The *Seahorse* foundered near Brownstown Head, close to Tramore Bay, Co. Waterford, and the *Boadicea* came ashore in Holeopen Bay to the west of the Old Head of Kinsale, Co. Cork; in all, 565 lost their lives. The *Lord Melville* carried 470 soldiers when it was driven onto rocks further west in Courtmacsherry Bay but was more fortunate, as the majority on board made it to land safely with help from the local inhabitants. The loss of shipping around the British Isles in the nineteenth century is incredible, and in the year 1868 alone an astonishing 2,131 vessels were damaged at sea, of which 629 were total losses. This, however, was a century during which tens of thousands of commercial craft of every kind plied their trade around these islands.

On 28 April 1859 the American emigrant ship *Pomona* (described in some reports as *Pomone*) was wrecked on Blackwater Bank, near Tuskar Rock, off Carnsore Point,

Co. Wexford. The death toll was 424, and when divers examined the hull they discovered about 300 corpses below deck. It was rumoured that the captain, who did not survive, had battened down the hatches.

Further north, off Bray Head, Co. Wicklow, in 1875 the ironclad battleship HMS *Vanguard*, part of a fleet of five vessels in line ahead, was rammed by her sister ship HMS *Iron Duke* during thick fog and sank in a little over an hour; all those on board were saved. The wreck is virtually intact and lying on her starboard side at a 45° list. The masts lie on the seabed and all of the huge muzzle-loading guns are still in position.

In 1915 Roger Casement persuaded the German government to send arms and ammunition to Ireland for use in the planned 1916 Rising. A cargo ship was refitted, disguised as the Norwegian ship *Aud*, and set out for Ireland, where it was to rendezvous with a German submarine with Casement on board. Things did not go according to plan, however, and the *Aud* was intercepted by a Royal Navy sloop, which ordered it to proceed to Queenstown. On the way it was scuttled by its captain and sank at the approach to Cork Harbour, with the loss of all its cargo.

The Cunard Line transatlantic passenger steamship *Carpathia* met its end off the east coast, when it was sunk by a German U-boat on 17 July 1918. This ship is famous for coming to the aid of the *Titanic* in 1912 and rescuing many of the passengers. In November 1986 the huge bulk carrier *Kowloon Bridge* left Quebec for Glasgow with 160,000 tons of iron ore. Her deck was damaged owing to heavy weather in mid-Atlantic and she sought shelter in Bantry Bay. Shortly afterwards she dragged her anchor and was forced out to sea, where she lost her rudder. At that stage all 22 crew abandoned ship and the helpless vessel drifted towards the coast, until she struck Stag Rocks near Baltimore, Co. Cork, and sank. It is the largest wreck by tonnage in the world.

There have been thousands of sinkings, but a book of this size can only describe a very small number. A halt must be made but the opportunity taken to pay tribute to the men of the Irish Merchant Navy, who braved the greatest hazards during the Second World War to bring essential supplies of food and fuel to their homeland. Although Ireland was neutral and its ships were clearly marked on their sides and decks with the tricolour and brightly lit at night, they were attacked on 41 occasions and seventeen were sunk by submarines, aircraft or mines. The greatest single loss was the 33 men who died on the cargo ship *Irish Pride*, torpedoed by a German U-boat on 16 November 1942 in the North Atlantic. By the end of the war 135 sailors had lost their lives and many more were wounded in a fleet that never had more than 800 men serving at any one time. Irish ships also saved 521 men of all nationalities whose

Memorial at City Quay, Dublin, to the Irish merchant seamen who died on duty during the Second World War.

ships had been sunk. The most remarkable rescue was by the motor vessel *Kerlogue*, homeward bound from Lisbon, which sailed into the aftermath of the sinking of the German destroyer *T26* at dawn on 29 December 1943. Hundreds of sailors were in the sea, many badly wounded, when the *Kerlogue* went to their aid, and ten hours later 168 survivors were on board, far exceeding the number of the crew. She eventually reached Cork, where the 164 men still alive were landed. One sometimes feels that the courage and sacrifice of these men, who had no means of defending themselves, are not fully appreciated.

13

SAFEGUARDING THE COAST

Up to the middle of the eighteenth century it is doubtful whether there was an official rescue service anywhere for vessels that came to grief at sea. When a ship was wrecked, the crew almost always relied on their own efforts to survive. If a ship sank just off the coast, those on shore would usually come to their assistance, but more often than not there was as much interest in the goods being washed ashore as in the lives of the sailors.

The situation greatly improved in the nineteenth century, when public opinion forced the authorities to take action and provide help for those who came to grief. Ireland was in the forefront, and the Dublin Ballast Board was set up in 1786 under the aegis of the Dublin Port Authority to oversee pilotage, the maintenance of buoys and safety and navigation in Dublin Bay. They also set up one of the earliest organised life-saving services in Europe, with lifeboat stations at Clontarf (1801), Sandycove (1803), Pigeon House (1804), Sutton (1805), Bulloch (1816) and Poolbeg (1825).

A major turning point was the founding of the Royal National Lifeboat Institution in 1824, since when it has played a major role in the saving of life at sea. There are 34 stations in Ireland, two of which are based inland—at Lough Derg, Co. Tipperary, and Enniskillen, Co. Fermanagh. In 2010 Irish lifeboats launched 976 times and rescued 1,008 people. With the introduction of the new Tamar-class lifeboat Ireland has one of the most advanced rescue vessels operational anywhere.

Heroic rescues have been carried out during the past 200 years, many by shelterless rowing lifeboats, and scores of lifeboatmen have sacrificed their lives. In Ireland the greatest single loss was on Christmas Eve 1895, when the Kingstown lifeboat *Civil Service No. 7* went to the rescue of the barque *Palme*, which was breaking up on Merrion Strand. As it approached the wreck, a massive wave engulfed the lifeboat, throwing all fifteen crew into the water, where they died from drowning or exposure. As a result, fifteen women became widows and 36 children fatherless. The public funeral was the largest in the history of Kingstown (Dun Laoghaire).

A drawing of the *Original*, the first purpose-built lifeboat in the British Isles, designed and built by Henry Greathead (1757–1818) (courtesy of the Royal National Lifeboat Institution, Poole, Dorset).

The second-worst disaster was on 20 February 1914, when the *Helen Blake* of Fethard, Co. Wexford, went to the rescue of the three-masted schooner *Mexico*. The latter had been totally wrecked on Keeragh Island, and as the lifeboat neared the vessel she was struck by heavy seas, thrown against the rocks and smashed to pieces, killing nine of the fourteen men on board. The Rosslare and Wexford lifeboats were also involved, and the former saved the lives of the men on the *Mexico*.

A memorial was erected a few years ago at the headquarters of the RNLI in Poole, Dorset, to the 778 voluntary lifeboatmen from every part of the British Isles who died during rescue operations—a remarkable story of sacrifice by unpaid volunteers.

The greatest safety measure taken in nineteenth-century Ireland was the building of lighthouses on a grand scale. Although the light at Hook Head, Co. Wexford, is one of the oldest in the British Isles, having been built in 1172, only a small number were erected over the next six centuries, with disastrous consequences for shipping. In 1810, under the auspices of the Dublin Port Authority, a plan was devised to erect lighthouses wherever they were required, and by the end of the century 60 had been built, all of which are still in use today. This was a huge undertaking and one of the greatest achievements of Victorian Ireland. All of the sites were, by their nature, isolated, storm-swept, exposed and dangerous, whilst the working conditions were harsh and extremely difficult, bearing in mind the technology at the time. The famous Fastnet Rock off County Cork took seven years to complete, and its construction was described as heroic when it became operational in 1903. Eleven more lighthouses came into existence in the twentieth century, some of which replaced earlier lights. Probably the best known is the Kish light-vessel off the south County Dublin coast, which was towed into position in 1965.

Lighthousemen were a special breed and had a lonely and sometimes dangerous working life. This was especially the case for those on uninhabited islands, who could be cut off from the mainland for weeks at a time in stormy weather. During the latter part of the twentieth century, however, all lighthouses became automated and lighthouse men became redundant owing to the rapid advances in marine technology, especially satellite navigation through the global positioning system (GPS). Even the fog-horn (previously the fog-bell) has been abolished. A certain romanticism has been lost as a result but lighthouses continue to play a vital role in marine safety. They have been under the control of the Commissioners of Irish Lights since 1867.

The invention of the helicopter in the middle of the twentieth century was another great blessing to seafarers and people in difficulty along the shoreline. It can

Fastnet lighthouse, Co. Cork.

reach those in trouble much more quickly than any boat and is able to operate where no other form of rescue is possible. It also has a greater range and the ability to move those seriously injured to hospital rapidly, in addition to providing first aid on board. In combination with lifeboats it provides a very effective rescue service. The crews of helicopters also take great risks and we remember the four members of the Air Corps who lost their lives on a rescue mission off the Waterford coast in 1999.

The Irish Coast Guard is responsible for the coordination of maritime search and rescue operations in the Republic of Ireland. Under its control are, *inter alia*, SAR helicopters, the RNLI, Community Rescue Boats of Ireland and the Irish Cave Rescue Organisation. Where the occasion arises, the Air Corps and Naval Service in the Republic and the Royal Navy and Royal Air Force in Northern Ireland also play their part. Despite all these services and the availability of 24-hour weather forecasts, lives are lost every year, many owing to carelessness and failure to obey simple rules. Nevertheless, by comparison with the eighteenth and nineteenth centuries the waters around Ireland are a much safer place.

Defending the coast.

BIBLIOGRAPHY

Automobile Association Touring Guide to Ireland (Dublin, *c.* 1950).

Jonathan Beaumont, *Rails to Achill* (Aberystwyth, 2002).

Edward J. Bourke, *Shipwrecks of Ireland* (Stroud, 2000).

Edward J. Bourke, *Bound for Australia* (Dublin, 2003).

Karl Brady (compiler), *Shipwreck Inventory of Ireland: Louth, Dublin, Meath and Wicklow* (Dublin, 2009).

Colin Breen and Wes Forsythe, *Boats and shipwrecks of Ireland* (Stroud, 2004).

Clare Journal and Ennis Advertiser (October 1907).

John De Courcy Ireland, *Wreck and rescue on the east coast of Ireland* (Dun Laoghaire, 1983).

John De Courcy Ireland, *History of Dun Laoghaire Harbour* (Dublin, 2001).

Denis Downey, *Next parish America* (Skibbereen, 2000).

John Eagle, *Ireland's lighthouses* (Cork, 2010).

Niall Fallon, *The Armada in Ireland* (London, 1978).

Frank Forde, *The long watch* (Dublin, 1981).

Freeman's Journal (November 1807).

Freeman's Journal (24/25 September 1884).

R. Gardiner and Dan Van Der Vat, *The riddles of the* Titanic (London, 1995).

Adrian Gilbert, *The encyclopaedia of warfare* (Hoo, 2002).

Paul Henry, *An Irish portrait* (London, 1951).

David Howarth, *The voyage of the Armada* (Glasgow, 1981).

Irish National Maritime Search and Rescue Framework (2010).

Irish Times (24/25/26/27 September 1884).

Irish Times (15/16/18 June 1894).

Irish Times (2/3/4 February 1953).

Irish Times (7 February 2009).

Irish Weekly Independent (23 June 1894).

J. Lennox Kerr, *The great storm* (London, 1954).

Brian Lalor (ed.), *The encyclopaedia of Ireland* (Dublin, 2003).

Richard Larn, *Shipwrecks of Great Britain and Ireland* (London, 1981).

Nicholas Leach, *The Lifeboat Service in Ireland* (Stroud, 2005).

Philip Lecane, *Torpedoed* (Penzance, 2005).

Bill Long, *Bright light, white water* (Dublin, 1993).

Cormac F. Lowth, 'Shipwrecks around Dublin Bay', *Dublin Historical Record* (Spring 2002).

David Lyons, *Ireland* (London, 2004).

Theresa McDonald, *Achill* (I.A.S. Publications, 1997).

Fraser G. MacHaffie, *The short sea route* (Prescot, 1975).

Enda McLaughlin, *Memoir for the* Wasp (Dublin, 1989).

Tom MacSweeney, *Seascapes* (Cork, 2008).

Senan Molony, Lusitania—*an Irish tragedy* (Cork, 2004).

Sheila Mulcahy, *A gallant barque* (Tralee, 1999).

Patrick O'Sullivan, *The* Lusitania—*unravelling the mysteries* (Cork, 1998).

Brian Patterson, 'An Irishman's Diary', *Irish Times* (24 July, 2008).

Peter Pearson, *Between the mountains and the sea* (Dublin, 1998).

Diana Preston, *Wilful murder—the sinking of the* Lusitania (London, 2002).

Robert Stenuit, *Treasures of the Armada* (Bath, 1972).

Roy Stokes, *Death in the Irish Sea* (Cork, 1998).

The Leon XIII *Centenary Magazine 2007* (Quilty, 2007).